Grace for Muslims?

Grace for Muslims?

– the journey from fear to faith

Steve Bell

Authentic

A catalogue record for this book is available from the British Library
ISBN-13: 978-1-85078-719-8

Cover design by fourninezero design.
Printed in Great Britain by J.F.Print, Sparkford

To Jack & Monica (Abu wa Um Philip)
See you in the morning

Contents

Foreword

by Brother Andrew

Recently someone who was working with Arab Muslims in a refugee camp in the Middle East shared her story with me. When she tried to describe this work to her home church an elder reacted angrily. 'I don't understand how you can work with these people, they don't deserve it.' Her answer was straightforward: 'You are right, but neither do we.'

I recalled this incident when I read Steve Bell's book *Grace for Muslims?* It is true; Muslims don't deserve the good news of the gospel but neither do Christians. It is grace that God came in Christ to share his love with all of us.

For many Christians it seems difficult to use 'grace' and 'Muslim' in the same context. This is not surprising after 9/11 when the only Islam many people see is angry and militant. *Grace for Muslims?* does not deny the darker side of Islam or the groups that are willing to fight the West with religious zeal. It does not deny the many areas of the world where Christians are put under pressure by Muslims; neither does it absolutize the extreme side of Islam either.

Steve Bell acknowledges the many faces of Islam and gives us the sort of multi-coloured and balanced picture of

Muslims that helps Christians to form relationships with them. Muslims deserve a little grace from Christians rather than bias based on prejudice. Steve encourages Christians to reflect this grace in their lives and attitudes towards Muslims. This is the strength of *Grace for Muslims?*

I am deeply touched and encouraged by this wonderful book by Steve and I would really like to endorse it. The book is not an abstract theory but a personal story which makes it easy for the reader to identify with. Steve shares how he was converted from grievance with Muslims to grace towards them. This results in fruitful lessons for Christians today. I pray that many Christians will read it and be touched by it.

Like any other part of the world, what the Islamic world needs is Christians that are being transformed into mirrors of grace and reflecting God's love for Muslims.

Brother Andrew
Open Doors International Study Centre
Harderwijk
The Netherlands
April 2006

Glossary
Word list and definitions

baraka	blessing
biram	an Islamic *'eîd* (feast) commemorating Abraham's sacrifice of his son
Charismatic	part of the evangelical wing of the church in any denomination, focused on spiritual renewal and gifts of the Spirit and an expressive worship style
Christian	1. Someone who trusts Jesus Christ for the forgiveness of their sin and their eternal salvation and who subsequently follows Jesus regardless of denominational allegiance or theological persuasion
	2. Also used to describe someone from a Christian community within a Muslim state e.g. the Christian community of Egypt (Coptic) or Pakistan
	3. Also used to refer to the notion of being nominally Christian e.g. Britain as a culturally Christian society or the assumption of Muslims that all westerners are 'Christian'
da'wa	Islamic mission, based on the Arabic word to invite
'eîd	an Islamic feast

Evangelical	a follower of Jesus Christ whose faith centres around the Gospel, a conversion experience and is committed to spreading the Gospel, includes the Pentecostal and Charismatic sectors of the church
fatwa	legal opinion given by a qualified Islamic theologian
al-Fâtiḥa	literally 'the opening', the first chapter of the Qur'an
Great Commission	the last command of Christ to take the Gospel to every person on Earth (Mt. 28:16-20; Lk. 24:45-49; Acts.1:6-8)
hâjj	pilgrimage to Mecca, the fifth pillar of Islam
halal	literally 'that which is loosed' from prohibition (i.e. lawful)
hijra	Muhammad's 'migration' from Mecca to Medina
iftâr	the breaking of fast meal during Ramadan
ikhwân al-muslimûn	'Muslim Brotherhood' (see definition under 'm')
îmâm	a recognized responsible and knowledgeable Muslim, leader of prayers
intefâda	literally 'uprising' (e.g. Palestinian struggle with Israeli government)
'îsa	the Qur'anic term for Jesus
îslâm	literally 'submission', the name of the religion
islâm	I use this also for the concept of a 'submitted' life (i.e. 'doing my *îslâm*')
jaâma'	literally 'gathering' (i.e. a mosque, also *masjid*)
jihâd	to struggle in the way of God spiritually or militarily
jihâdi	someone who resorts to violent forms of struggle in the way of God militarily
ka'âba	the cube shaped edifice in the Grand Mosque in Mecca

kalîma	the creedal statement 'There is no god but God and Muhammad is his Messenger'
kitâb al-muqaddas	the Holy Bible
al-Masîḥ	Christ
masjid	see 'mosque' (also *jaâma'*, gathering place for worship)
mikvah	Jewish ritual bath at conversion, precursor to Christian baptism
mission	any activity aimed at reaching beyond the needs of the local congregation to
	1. proclaim the gospel
	2. baptize and nurture new believers
	3. serve the whole need of people both spiritual and physical
	4. seek to transform unjust structures in society
	5. strive to safeguard and sustain the life of the earth
missiology	the academic study of missionary issues
missional church	a local church that exists for its non-members and is acting in accordance with its missionary nature
mosque	the English name for the Muslim meeting and prayer room
muezzin	person who performs the call to prayer from a minaret
muhâsaba	a definitive and agreed upon issue
mujâhid	someone who performs *jihâd*, particularly military struggle
mujâhideen	the plural of *mujâhid*
mu'min	a believer, a godly person
Muslîm	as a noun: someone who is born into the Muslim community
muslîm	as an adjective: denotes a quality (e.g. 'a *muslim* thing to do')
Muslîma	a female Muslim
Muslim brotherhoods	networks of militant Muslims who work for the defence of Islamic interests and are prepared to engage in violent *jihâd*

mûwlâna	a trainee mullah (i.e. senior Islamic scholar)
nabî	prophet
Pentecostal	part of the evangelical wing of the church, the experience of a 'second blessing' of the Spirit with the initial evidence of speaking in tongues and the manifestation of spiritual gifts
pluralism	the belief that society should give all minority groups (ethnic, religious, moral) the same distinction, thinking should be inclusive and all 'truths' are relative
post-modern	a worldview that deconstructs the past and affirms all truths as only a relative part of ultimate truth, an analytical view that all views are equally valid
qibla	direction of prayer towards Mecca
qur'ân	literally 'that which is recited', the holy book of Islam, also spelled Koran
ramadân	the ninth month of the Islamic calendar, fasting month
sâdaqa	the Muslim equivalent of freewill almsgiving
salât	prayer, the second pillar or practice in Islam
salvation history	the term used to describe the developing theme through the Bible from the Fall to the Cross i.e. God called a man (Abraham) to form a people (the Jews) to produce a Saviour (Jesus Christ) to save the world
sawm	fasting
Semitic	of the lineage of Shem, son of Noah including Jews, Arabs, Assyrians and Phoenicians
shahâda	confession, the first pillar of Islam 'There is no God . . .'
shalwâr kamees	the baggy pantaloons and shirt worn by Pakistanis
sharî'a law	the amalgamation of Qur'an, Hadith and legal opinions of Islamic scholars

shaykh	literally an elder, a title given to an Islamic scholar
shekinah	Hebrew, the supernatural luminosity of the divine presence
shia'a	the second largest Muslim group, mostly found in Iran and Iraq
shi'ite	the adjectival form of the noun *shia'a*
shi'i	another adjectival form of the noun *shia'a*
sîrat	literally a 'pathway' (i.e. in the desert to a watering hole)
sunni	the major Islamic group worldwide
ta'rîf	the alteration or corruption of scripture
takfîri	a *jihâdi* intent on suicide
tanzîl	literally 'to come down' (i.e. the revelation of the Qur'an)
tarîqa	literally 'pathway', used to describe spiritual mentoring
tawrât	the Jewish Torah (i.e. Old Testament Law and Prophets)
tâwḥid	oneness, unity of God
torah	the Jewish Old Testament with Law and Prophets
umma	literally 'community', used of the world-wide house of Islam
zabûr	the Qu'ranic name for the Psalms of David
zakât	the fourth Muslim practice i.e. giving (i.e. 2.5 per cent of disposable income)

Pronunciation guide
How to say the Arabic words

I have kept these symbols to a minimum, using them only for Arabic words or technical Islamic expressions. Wherever possible the names of people and places are spelled as in the press. The aim is to help readers pronounce the words as accurately as possible for the sake of a Muslim friend. Remember that Hebrew and Arabic have no capital letters.

Symbol used   English pronunciation

'   glottal stop as in the 'a' of 'apple' e.g. *qur'an (Koran)*
ḥ   aspirated like the breath used when cleaning glasses
<u>kh</u>   as used in the German guttural sound in the word 'Na<u>ch</u>t'
<u>dh</u>   as in 'th' when pronouncing '<u>th</u>ose'
ṣ   Arabic letter sâd – heavy with a flat tongue
ḍ   Arabic letter dâd – heavy with a flat tongue
'   indicating the Arabic letter *ayn* – not found in any western language
<u>gh</u>   like the French 'r'
q   Arabic *qâf* – not found in English, uvular as in 'k' but not 'kw'

Lengthened vowels:
â   as in 'aah'
î   as in 'eee'
û   as in 'ooo'
ř   prolonged rolled 'r' sound

Prelude
Grace or naïvety?

Is it possible to adopt a grace response to Muslims without being either theologically woolly or politically naïve?

This book argues that the answer is an emphatic yes!

By 'grace-response' I mean willingness to alter the default mechanism in our brains which causes us to fear the unfamiliar in another person; being prepared to give others the benefit of the doubt and make an effort to find out why they behave as they do. A grace response is willing to include the other person within the scope of God's love and the Great Commission of Jesus Christ, rather than imagining there is an exclusion clause which puts them beyond our concern. We do not stereotype all Catholics on the basis of the behaviour of the IRA, so why do we judge all Muslims on the basis of the behaviour of Al-Qaeda?

By 'Muslims' I mean the ordinary people who did not ask to be born into their community. These people differ, not just from us but from one another. This is due to factors such as race, culture, language, theology and politics. One Muslim told me that if you ask two Muslims a question, you will get three opinions. We are wrong to try and lump all Muslims together under the assumption that they are a monolithic group who all think the same way.

The majority of Muslims arrived in Britain with a 'live and let live' mentality. Many of the early immigrants came at the invitation of the government but became trapped by their economic circumstances. The second, third and even fourth generation of these immigrants are now struggling with feelings of marginalization and frustration, while the older generation feel disillusioned and resentful – all of which we will explore.

However, if we are going to avoid political naïveté we have to recognize the fact that not all Muslims are 'ordinary'. According to a recent Gallop poll, the majority of British Muslims (roughly sixty-five per cent) think that *shari'a* law would do a better job than a secular government, while the minority (about twenty-five per cent) are radicalized.[1] These people vary in the extremism of their views; some have little respect for common law and intend the West to be forcibly 're-educated' by Islam; others work subversively in an effort to use democracy in order to destroy democracy. It is the hard core of this category of Muslim who fly planes into buildings or carry bombs onto public transport systems. Such Muslims are equally loved by God but can hardly be called 'ordinary'.

Many people do not want to respond to Muslims with grace because of the common fear that all Muslims want to take political power, declare *shari'a* law at Westminster and abolish all other religions and democractic principles, including freedom of speech. One observer says that, 'It is obvious that for most Muslims in Britain, *da'wa* (mission) was never their motivation for coming to this country, nor was it the *raison d'être* of their remaining here. In fact it is usually Christians (rather than secularists) who raise the spectre of a potential takeover of this country by Muslims.'[2]

Some people misunderstand the concept of a grace response to Muslims, believing it to be an attempt to appease Muslims where they need challenging; this is not my meaning at all as we will see. Brother Andrew observes that grace can come to us more easily when we become more familiar with what drives the most hardened Islamist militant. He cites the sense of depression that affects militants in Palestine, causing them to see only their insurmountable social problems and the despair that they

will never defeat in battle those they hold responsible. This
state of affairs provokes them to evil deeds while their
religion only offers heaven to those who do enough good
deeds. For such Muslims, to die in violent *jihad* is the
ultimate 'good deed' and the only way they can be sure of
Paradise. Brother Andrew has met this kind of Muslim
and has said that 'they see no reason to live so they choose
the only reason to die'. He urges Christians to

> Go to the Muslims and tell them that they do not have to die
> because Jesus died for their sins. We will never win the
> encounter with Islam through discussions or sermons. We
> have to go and show them how Jesus can change people.[3]

This book takes the view that it is not the so-called 'expert'
but the ordinary Christian who is rubbing shoulders with
the ordinary Muslim in the work-a-day world. To help
such Christians, we go behind the disturbing headlines to
find that an Islamic 'threat' may not be the real issue at all.
We will also see that there are some unexpected positives
that the Muslim presence brings to the West, such as their
questioning of secular-humanism, something which our
culture has refused to hear from the church over the past
few decades. This is just one reason why Islam sits
uncomfortably in the West, which is tacitly extending an
invitation to Muslims to join it in its spiritual vagueness;
something many Muslims cannot and will not do.

Many Muslims react to western thinking on a number
of issues. To help us understand these issues we will hear
from Muslims who can help us. The veteran Iranian
journalist Amir Taheri provides a helpful insight into the
conflicting spread of attitudes among British Muslims.

> The loudest Islam is a political movement masquerading as a
> religion. Many mosques in Britain and throughout Europe,

have been transformed into political clubs where Palestine, Kashmir, Iraq and 'the misdeeds of Anglo-Saxon imperialism' have replaced issues of religious faith as the principal theme.[4]

Taheri goes on to show that the problem underlying the behaviour of radical British Muslims is that the true Islamic agenda in Britain has been hijacked because British Muslims 'have no religious grievances'. They come from homelands where there is a high level of sectarian feuding. In the West where they can 'practise religion with more freedom than in any Muslim-ruled country', they know such feuds cannot be continued. As a result, Muslim activists tend to minimise the religious aspects and emphasise the political issues which unite Muslims.

This book recognises the Jewish elements in Islam but rather than eulogise about them, we will find explanations for the contradiction posed by 'violent' and 'spiritual' Islam. However, we will also come to terms with the Old Testament theological and cultural characteristics that carried over into Islam. We will see how, in modern times, western Christians are more easily shocked by religious violence than our counterparts in the Middle Ages, because we have moved away from the Semitic mindset of our own faith. As a result, Christianity's Middle Eastern roots have become largely ignored, as the Roman tradition of Christianity became uncompromisingly western. In other words, the entire Middle East predictably developed its own form of Semitic (or eastern) spirituality – Islam. This form of Abramic faith gained momentum, despite having little access to the Bible. Islam had no difficulty sweeping up many societies that were enemies of the Roman Empire. This drift apart has given us the lines of religious divisions with Christianity, which is seen by Muslims as western, and Islam, which Muslims see as authentically eastern.[5]

This is why modern Muslims arrive in the West in our day looking like an Old Testament people. Muslims simply will not buy into some of our western ways; something that is incomprehensible to secularists. Christians have a real role to play here because they can understand and show secular Britons how to relate appropriately to Muslims.

In the current climate it would be all too easy to write yet another alarmist Christian book about the dangers of political Islam; its human rights abuses and the repressive social systems which exist in many Muslim countries. Some of these books have their place and it would be naïve to dispute the facts raised in them. However, the title *Grace for Muslims* indicates that I propose to show how we can hold these negatives in tension with the positives we will discover. There is a third way between being a cynical armchair critic of Muslims and a naïve wishful thinker who hopes things will turn out all right in the end as future generations of western Muslims drop their core values and become culturally assimilated.

One Christian who balanced political realism with a gracious attitude towards Muslims was St Francis of Assisi who wandered around various Middle Eastern lands as an apostle of grace at a time when Europeans distrusted Muslims. His well known prayer becomes even more poignant when we read it against the backdrop of the Islamic cultures he moved in.

Lord make me an instrument of your peace; where there is hatred, let me sow love; where there is injury, pardon; where there is doubt, faith; where there is despair, hope, and where there is sadness, joy.

Divine Master, grant that I may not so much seek to be consoled as to console, to be understood as to understand, to be loved as to love.

For it is in giving that we receive. It is in pardoning that we are pardoned, and in dying that we are born to eternal life.

The answer to this prayer can only be possible through the grace of God; this is something that is badly needed by many western Christians who are struggling with an attitude problem towards Muslims.

As I have written this book at a time when Muslims are, once again, generally mistrusted. I am seeking to strike a balance by focusing on the less reported positive situations where grace is being extended both to Muslims and (startlingly) *from* Muslims to others. My driving passion is that western Christians should understand the divine strategy that is being worked out and become part of the answer to St Francis' prayer.

I have tried to show that the prayer is already being modelled around the world. For example through the book we will see that . . .

Love is being sown into hatred in Nigeria: in chapter five we see Muslim and Christian neighbours hiding one another in their homes in order to protect each other during inter-communal violence.

Pardon is being sown into injury in Israel: in chapter five we see a Palestinian Muslim family, whose son was killed by Israeli soldiers, donate their dead son's organs to a hospital in order to save the lives of Jewish children; and British Christians give out red roses to Muslims as they leave Watford mosque on the first Friday after 9/11.

Faith is being sown into doubt around the world: in the second interlude chapter we find that God is calling Muslims to follow Jesus Christ in greater numbers than at any other time in history. Other Muslims are finding their way to the West where they have the opportunity to 'reach out for him and find him' (Acts 17:27).

Light is being sown into darkness: we dispel the myths about Muslims by clarifying the difference between 'Islam' the politico-religious system and 'Muslims'; as people born into that system.

Hope is being sown into despair: in chapter six we glimpse the prospect for a future after the demise of multi-culturalism. We see the presence of dispersed Muslims in the West not as a divine mistake but as a development that is providentially within the sovereignty of God in human history (Eph. 1:11).

Finally *joy is being sown into the sadness* caused by violence where Islam has become the common denominator in suffering and bloodshed. I share my own struggle with the various issues presented by Islam. After nearly three decades, and against some real odds, my journey has brought me from *fear* of Muslims to *faith* for them – with love (Gal. 5:6).

It is when the prayer of Francis of Assis is answered through us that we will find ourselves able to 'bear all things, believe all things, hope all things and endure all things' (1 Cor. 13:7 NKJV). This is a biblical response rather than a human reaction to Muslims.

To answer the question posed at the beginning of this Prelude, I ask hard questions of both western societies and Muslim societies; Christians as well as Muslims. As westerners we can find it unpalatable to be confronted with the cultural 'log' that is in our own eye, before addressing whatever can be found in the eye of our Muslim neighbour (Mt. 7:3). Patterns of wrong-doing by western societies past and present are included in order to help foster an attitude in us that makes us prepared to ask how Christians and Muslims can face their common cultural faults and explore solutions together.

The book goes further than many others by explaining how to do something about the Muslims who have come to live in our postcode. My aim is to help you develop a more nuanced understanding of Islam, discover God's heart for Muslim people and what he might be saying to western society through the Muslim presence; and to show how Christians can use the existing links between Judaism and Islam to share the good news about Jesus with Muslims, in a more appropriate way.

God is asking western followers of Jesus to be available to Muslims who are becoming his 'eastern followers'. The book will show you how we can help such eastern followers to do so in ways that are culturally appropriate to them. In order to do this we need to pray with Francis of Assisi 'Divine Master, grant that I may not so much seek to be understood as to understand.'

If you are prepared to *serve* Muslims in this way – read on.

Notes

1. Smith J, *Is it time to confront?* (CIS Bulletin: London College of Theology, 2003), p13-14. An ICM opinion poll also came up with the figure of 40 per cent support by British Muslims for the introduction of *shari'a* law in Britain while 91 per cent of British Muslims said they feel loyal to Britain (*Sunday Telegraph*, 19 February 2006, p1).
2. Musk B, *Kissing Cousins* (Oxford: Monarch Books, 2005), p237.
3. Brother Andrew addressing the fiftieth anniversary of Open Doors in Neidernhausen, Germany (*Friday Fax* 48, 9 December 2005), fridayfax@bufton.net.
4. Taheri A., We don't do God, we do Palestine and Iraq (*Sunday Times:* 12 February 2006), p12.
5. Ralph Winter, *Mission Frontiers* (US Center for World Mission: Jan-Feb 2006), p4.

Chapter 1

Grace calling

'From my kitchen sink I can see to the ends of the earth.'

It was a Wednesday lunchtime in 1979 and my weekly lunch date with my first spiritual mentor, Mrs Snook, a matronly Christian with a vivacious personality, sharp mind and an acute spiritual perception. 'I can see them all,' she continued.

She was looking wistfully at the brick wall of the house opposite the kitchen window. I realized that she had gone off on one of her tangents. She meant that her geographical location had no bearing on her spiritual reach. Margaret Snook had never possessed a passport or journeyed further than the Isle of Wight on holiday; yet in prayer she frequently travelled the world through her connections with Christian leaders and mission partners.

I met Margaret just after my conversion in my late teenage years. My decision to follow Christ triggered a series of supernatural encounters, including a vision of him, dreams and even being touched by an invisible being whom I assumed was an angel. These experiences gave me an affinity with Muslims who often experience the supernatural as part of their journey to Christ.

I became a member of a church that exposed me to the Great Commission, in which Jesus commanded his followers to become his witnesses in Jerusalem (locally), Judea/Samaria (regionally and nationally) and to the ends of the earth (globally). I understood from this that any Bible-based church should engage in all three zones at the same time. This pattern became my experience because the 'ends of the earth' had come to live in my 'Jerusalem'. I became a cross-cultural witness for Christ without leaving my postcode.

At that time I was living in student digs opposite Trent Fields in Nottingham. One day a circus set up on part of this green-belt and I noticed that the workers were foreign. I plucked up courage and wandered across to find out where they were from. One man told me in broken English they were 'Maghrebi'. He said this with a gargling sound on the 'gh'. I had no idea what he meant so I went away and found out it was Arabic for 'Moroccan'. I contacted Lifewords in London[1] and ordered a supply of Arabic Gospels of Luke. I returned to the circus caravans where I was made welcome with a glass of mint tea. I asked if they would like to read something in their own language and passed the Gospels round the group of young men, who scrutinized them carefully. Three of them said nothing, two of them thanked me and the last one kissed his copy before putting it in his breast pocket. I thanked them for the tea and left.

I had taken my first step in cross-cultural mission within a few hundred yards of my flat. I found that local churches seemed equipped to get the good news about Jesus to indigenous Britons but were not even thinking about visitors such as these Moroccans, let alone actively reaching them?

Another opportunity for local cross-cultural witness presented itself when I started my probationary year as a school teacher. My first post was at Mundella Comprehensive – in a highly multi-racial part of Nottingham called The Meadows. It was an economic priority area and the scene of race riots in 1980. I was the only black teacher. Black and Asian pupils worried about the mounting tensions confided in me before something was about to happen, so the police could be alerted.

Forty-five per cent of the pupils were Asian and my first impression of them was how smart, clean and well turned out most of them were. On the whole, they were also harder working, better behaved and under better parental control than the other pupils. I never had to tell Asian pupils, whether from a Hindu, ethnic Christian or Muslim background, to show respect to members of staff. Their instinct was to stand up whenever an adult walked into the room, in keeping with Old Testament practice (Lev. 19:32). This contrasted with my indigenous white pupils, particularly when hormones were kicking in and they were turning into stroppy teenagers.

I found Muslims to be ordinary human beings when I talked to Asian parents about their children. Take, for instance, my first parents' evening just after the Easter holidays when I had made my first trip to Pakistan. The trip included driving from Islamabad to Peshawar and also a train ride from Peshawar to Lahore, during which a group of students engaged me in a long discussion about Islam and Christianity. I will never forget the look on the parents' faces. It was a connection which caused them to warm to me and I to them. The fact that I had done the Peshawar/Lahore train journey delighted some of them who had been born and raised in villages along that route.

I understood why these immigrants preferred to live in clan ghettos in the UK. Most of them had come to Britain with the notion of bettering themselves in the former colonial mother-country which was happy to welcome them into the less popular jobs but showed almost total incomprehension of their religious outlook. The polite inference was that it would have been better if they had left their religion behind. Pakistani parents found Britain alien, which is why they lived in close proximity to one another. It safeguarded their identity and gave mutual support.

One frustrated parent told me 'I wish they wouldn't just criticize us. Why don't they see what we can offer – moral and spiritual values?' It came as a surprise to hear a Muslim express a sense of spiritual obligation to contribute something to the flagging profile of faith in Britain. This sort of encounter made me realize that not all Muslims think the same thing, like soldier ants working towards some hidden agenda.

These Pakistani parents were so different in language, dress, mentality, food and culture to the Moroccans I had met at the circus on Trent Fields some months earlier. Each ethnic group I came across were a separate entity, rather than being one monolithic whole. The Moroccans would find the Pakistanis quite foreign. Their only point of connection would be the beliefs and historic connections of their common religion. I could only liken this to the English language being the main point of connection between a Briton and a Pakistani; and even then the two forms of English differ significantly. In the same way, the Islam practised in North Africa and the Indo-Pakistan sub-continent are different. I became intrigued by the worldwide loosely inter-connected network of Muslims who gravitated to their own group for security.

It was during my time at Mundella School in 1980 that I first experienced the love of God expressing itself through me to Muslims. I was aware of the strategic opportunity that teachers and other civil servants have as they mix naturally with Muslims in the West. If only Christians could break down their own negative stereotypes about

Muslims and in turn be open to help break down the misconceptions that Muslims have about white people.

This 'regions beyond' outlook (2 Cor. 10:16) was a feature of my home church on the edge of Nottingham. This meant that overseas mission workers who were linked to the church would encourage young nationals who were coming to the UK for study to come to Nottingham and join us. Even in the late 1970s this suburban mono-cultural congregation had a multi-cultural fringe to its thriving youth activities. We welcomed believing students from both the Christian and Muslim communities of Iran, Cyprus, Jordan, Nigeria, Pakistan and Turkey. I remember one earnest white youth asking an educated Iranian student from Muslim background whether Iran had the electricity to enjoy colour TV yet. Of course the student's wealthy family had colour TV well before it was widely available in the UK.

The 'regions beyond' ethos also took me into my Judea and Samaria regionally and nationally as I began to take up invitations to speak to church groups in various parts of the UK. Eventually my activities took me to the ends of the earth globally. This is where Mrs Snook came in: an intercessor who played an important part in my 'going global' phase.

I joined several summer mission teams to a North African country. One day I got into serious difficulties at passport control where border guards demanded to confiscate my passport; when I refused they proceeded to beat me. I could have been arrested and imprisoned.

When I arrived home in Nottingham, I called on Margaret Snook, who said, 'What was going on at four o'clock on the afternoon of Tuesday 18 August, UK time?' She had been alerted by the Spirit of God to pray for me at the precise time of the incident at the border. She advised me always to have a vision greater than the task in hand.

The task in hand for me was to become a qualified teacher and the greater vision was to live and be a witness for Jesus in the Arabic-speaking world.

During my final year of teacher training I was awarded a scholarship to study theology in the Middle East. In the late 1970s the Lebanese civil war was still on, so the only theological college that was not either liberal or being bombed was the Presbyterian Evangelical Seminary in Cairo. My plan was to do a one-year course before teaching English as a foreign language.

I arrived in Egypt in early September 1981 at the same time as Prince Charles and Princess Diana were there on honeymoon. It felt like I had arrived at the ends of the earth and I understood Abraham better because he too had left the security of his own land, culture and family to go to a land God showed him (Gen. 12:1). I walked out of Cairo International Airport into the hot evening atmosphere where I was surrounded by a jostling throng of people meeting people, hugging and kissing. Hordes of taxi-drivers touted for business and I scanned the mass of humanity for a glimpse of the people who were supposed to be meeting me.

It seemed that all my worldly belongings were in my suitcase. It was an exciting experience: yet it was also scary because it gave me that sense of vulnerability that inevitably comes with leaving the security of familiar surroundings and moving to a place that is so strange, it might as well be another planet. I thought my journey of faith was now over – in reality the adventure had barely begun.

Notes

1. Lifewords (formerly Scripture Gift Mission), Radstock House, 3 Eccleston Street, London SW1W 9LZ, tel: 020 7730 2155, www.lifewords.info.

Chapter 2

Defining grace

People who love interpret the facts about the one they love much more accurately than those who do not love. Because our eyes have seen badly we have only noticed the darker aspects.
John Chrysostom

My first six months in Egypt were a honeymoon period where everything was new, colourful and exciting. I saw the teeming millions who thronged the Cairo streets and realized that the likelihood of any of these Muslims hearing the good news about Jesus was far less than it was in the UK.

About a month after arriving in Cairo I started my scholarship at the Evangelical Theological Seminary, where I studied for a year. This was a fascinating place in which I befriended students from Egypt and the Sudan. This was where a personal journey into the grace of God would begin. Until now I had only understood grace as a theological idea which reassured my mind but had not reached my heart. I was in the place that Dietrich Bonhöeffer spoke about when he said, 'Cheap grace means grace as a doctrine, a principle, a system. Costly grace is the sanctuary of God.'[1] Grace sustained Bonhöeffer all the way to the gallows as a martyr under Nazi rule in wartime Germany. I needed this sort of sustaining grace in order to press through with God in my new and strange environment.

I rented my first apartment in the Heliopolis area near the airport. It was just under the flight path of the inbound flights arriving direct from Saudi Arabia. Culture shock began to set in. It was how I imagined it must be for people withdrawing from an addictive substance – my addiction was my Britishness. After six months I was gasping for the familiar air of English culture. Only now did I start to get an inkling of what 'culture' is and how it shapes our assumptions, instincts and even our bodily reflexes.

I was in an Arabic-speaking society where I had to learn how to talk all over again. It felt like a regression to a second childhood and I was frustrated that I could not express myself as well as Egyptian children. They could communicate fluently while I, a twenty-five-year-old man, could not.

In the UK I had been a big fish in the small pond of a local church but among Cairo's seventeen million people, I became a small fish in a vast ocean. I lost the security of having a defined status; a bereavement that made me vulnerable to loss of confidence and low self-worth. Anger would surface over silly things, such as people pushing in at the front of a queue because they knew the person who was serving.

Then there was the general stress of life in Cairo, thought to be the most densely populated city on earth. This has earned it the nickname 'The New York of the Middle East'. The city lies in a geographic depression that looks like a dust bowl from the air. Heavily polluted air hangs over it and living in Cairo is equal to smoking twenty cigarettes a day, according to the World Health Organization.

Culture shock

My insecurities were exposed because my Christianity had been like a spiritual version of the Protestant work ethic. It was more about *achieving* than *receiving*. My faith was driven by a sense of duty. My self-worth had come from my work, my identity had come from my activity and my sense of personal value had come from my role. I needed to discover that grace is not about *doing* but *resting* in what Christ has already done for me.

God waited for my strength to become exhausted then started work on me, using an Islamic society to take me apart. My ego took a battering, which resulted in a personal crisis. I faced the options of returning to England or learning to live in the grace of God. I am grateful to Jerry Bridges who summed up my experience perfectly when he said . . .

We are all damaged goods. Conditions are put on our self-worth e.g. 'You are good IF . . .' We may need to recover from 'toxic parenting' from sincere parents who were, them-selves, subject of 'toxic parenting' right back to Eden. Some Christians exchange 'toxic parenting' for 'toxic Christianity' i.e. self-effort to be what you're not. Without an experience of the grace of God we are vulnerable to insecurity, inferiority, jealousy, perfectionism, lack of self-worth, fear of failure and emotional exhaustion.[2]

These issues should have been dealt with before arriving in another culture. The result was two broken engagements and a lot of general emotional turbulence throughout this period.

In Arab societies, single men in their late twenties are not readily understood. I was offered brides by two well meaning families – one Christian, the other Muslim. It was a shock to me to find that conversations would often begin with the following questions from relative strangers – 'What's your name?' 'How old are you?' 'Are you married?' 'Why not?' 'How much do you earn?' and 'What rent do you pay for your apartment?' These questions were asked roughly in that order and they reflected the desire of Egyptians to place me appropriately in their complex social system.

Middle Eastern culture tends to segregate the sexes until marriage which meant I found myself in a society oriented towards homosexuality; something that is publicly denied but privately practised, not necessarily out of sexual orientation but as a recreational activity that provides sexual release for young men before they get married. I found this threatening because I, as a westerner, could not read the non-verbal signals that the locals understood. How was I to navigate my way around the holding of hands, kissing on both cheeks when greeting and leave-taking or the general tactile behaviour among men? An American colleague, who was also a mission partner, had to be sent home by his organization after slipping into a homosexual relationship with a Palestinian student he taught. I was once alone in a lift with a Gulf Arab who sexually propositioned me. He carried on all the way down from the sixth to the ground floor. He would not take 'No' for an answer and followed me almost all the way home before he gave up.

When I arrived in Egypt the country was under martial law after the assassination of President Anwar Sadat.

This meant that we had to live with constant security considerations. I was advised by Muslim friends to shave off a goatee beard I had because it was seen as a political statement and people were being arrested for wearing them. Western mission colleagues were put out of the country at irregular intervals so we had to learn to live with the police informers who were watching everything.

After the turbulent honeymoon period, I found myself returning to normality; I began to bond with my adoptive culture. By the end of the process my world was well and truly upside-down. Egypt had become home to me while the UK had become alien. My relationship with the land of my birth began to change; it has never been the same since.

Prepared for grace

The culture shock prepared me well for grace. It brought me to the place where I realized that I had been serving the 'work of the Lord' rather than the 'Lord of the work'. The cream of my energy therefore needed redirecting to *enjoy* relationship rather than to *do* ministry. I suspected that God had brought me to the Middle East in order to do something for me, rather than anything I could do for Egyptians.

Illness prepared me even further for grace when I contracted a viral infection that caused what the medics called a 'febrile episode'. The same illness killed a young Frenchman who picked it up at the same time as me. The condition caused violent night sweats and rigours (uncontrollable shaking) and I lost nearly half my body weight. I became too sick to be moved to hospital so a Christian doctor treated me at my lodgings while local Christians changed my bed linen and tended to my practical needs. I felt humbled when a western professional who attended our church and whose Christianity I had doubted (and said so) came to visit me and was entirely loving. This was an added pressure because grace was now being modelled for me.

During my convalescence I read the story of David Watson, the evangelical Anglican minister who came to treasure terminal cancer as a gift that brought him into closer relationship with God. I wept as I read these words

> God showed me that all my preaching, writing and other ministry was absolutely nothing compared to my love relationship with Him. In fact my sheer busyness had squeezed out the close intimacy I had known with Him.[3]

This was the turning point; I gave up trying to be the heroic full-time Christian worker. I stopped trying to operate out of a sense of the *ideal* me and came to terms with the *real* me. Henri Nouwen helped me when he said, 'The need for a heroic self-image is the biggest barrier to service for Christ . . . When I have nothing to lose I have nothing to defend. Only then can I have everything to give.'[4]

In search of biblical grace

During my two-month period of convalescence, I spent time reading the Bible more carefully in order to establish the facts about God's grace, which I was grasping for the first time in my life. First I saw that God's grace is the core disposition of God himself and therefore a synonym for the love that is God (1 Jn. 4:8-11,16). I realized that I should expect grace to be the consistent pattern of God's behaviour. I saw that grace is multi-dimensional because it is a noun, a verb and an adjective, all at the same time.

It is what God *is*, what he is *like*, as well as being what he *does*. Martin Luther called grace God's *opus proprium* i.e. 'proper work', a reference to the fact that grace is the motivation of everything God thinks, says or does.[5]

Next I saw that grace is the consistent theme of the Bible to which every other theme relates, either directly or indirectly. The earliest instances of grace emerge in the book of Genesis and not the Gospel of Matthew, as I had assumed. I noticed that even the Law of Moses was only an interim grace-provision, setting the moral standards to which God's grace was to lift us in Christ. In other words, Old Testament law was an initial provision of covenant love as a temporary arrangement en route to the culmination in New Covenant grace (Gal. 3:24). Grace is therefore the 'wisdom of God'; it is superior to the law in the sense that it invades human nature and accomplishes in us what the law could not (1 Cor. 2:7, 10; Rom. 8:3-4).

The words used in the Old Testament to encapsulate the multi-faceted nature of grace include 'generosity', 'favour', 'pardon', 'mercy', 'goodness', 'long-suffering', 'kindness' and 'tender mercies'. The New Testament also speaks of God's 'love', 'mercy', 'grace gift' as well as his 'compassion'. Jesus was the culmination and not the initiation of grace. In fact, the whole plot of the Bible shows grace like a partially concealed thread that weaves its way through the ages until it is finally revealed in Christ. I now understood grace to be the divine stoop of God to save us and make us whole (Jer. 29:11).

In the same way that light refracts from a multi-faceted jewel, so grace is the love of God in action towards undeserving humankind.[6] We can forgive but only God can forgive and forget sin (Is. 43:25; Ps. 103:12). God's grace in us can enable us to forgive ourselves where necessary and then forgive others.

I noticed too that God's grace gives people the benefit of the doubt and is touched by the needs of others – even people like me. I concluded that grace is God looking beyond fault and seeing need. I was fascinated by the way God's grace absorbs sin like moral blotting paper (Is. 1:18; 44:22; Acts 3:19 AV). It has the capacity to soak up even my mess. So grace may not make me forget the past wrongs done against me but I became convinced that it certainly can release me to attach new meaning to those memories.[7] This was the key to extending grace to Muslims if I chose to do so. Grace is therefore an aspect of the divine love that wants to constrain us all to 'always trust, always hope' and 'always persevere' (1 Cor. 13:7).

It was this sort of insight that catapulted me way beyond the surface definitions I had been taught, such as grace is 'unmerited favour' or the acrostic

G – God's
R – riches
A – at
C – Christ's
E – expense.

Although these were neat definitions which can be helpful, I found that they were more like descriptions of what grace *does* rather than definitions of what grace *is*. They describe grace in *action* but not grace in *essence* – the *fruit* rather than the *root*.

Grace and the Apostle Paul

I found that for the Apostle Paul, grace is not just a theological proposition but a spiritual impetus that energizes and motivates the believer in daily experience.

'His grace to me was not without effect. No, I worked harder than all of them – yet not I, but the grace of God that was with me' (1 Cor. 15:10). Paul taught that grace is an internal dynamic of the Spirit of God that provides the lift and forward thrust to serve Christ (Rom. 1:5; 12:6; 15:15; Gal. 2:9; Eph. 3:2,7). This experience is more than just a worthy way to think *about* Christ theologically, it is the way for us to live *in* Christ experientially. The New Church leader Terry Virgo described the reality of practical everyday grace when he likened it to the horizontal escalators at airports

> I often pass through airports, extremely grateful for the moving pavements that I find there. If I have a heavy case I am happy to rest and let the machine carry me and the case along. Often, however, these wonderful automatic walkways are found within the airport before one has collected one's luggage. So there is no need to pause. I can stride along, stretching legs that have been confined on the journey – and what a pace I can do as I take advantage of the momentum afforded me by the walkway.[8]

Grace and the Muslim

As a young Christian, I had developed a lazy way of thinking. To me, other religions were darkness with no redeeming features. I preferred their complexity to be simplified so that a black and white conclusion about them could be reached easily. I was also influenced by the poor adherence to Islam by some Muslims; something a Muslim could say about some Christians. My opinion was based on an emotional reaction to Islam, especially fundamentalism and also on the negative attitude of Christians whom I assumed knew what they were talking about. As a result I was unable to see through the irrational arguments and appreciate the areas in Islam that are actually biblical.

I had never really bothered to study the religion, so I had some catching up to do in order to reconcile what I had been told Muslims believe and what I found Muslims actually believe. I knew just enough to be critical but not enough to explain why. I needed to stop giving false testimony against my neighbour (Ex. 20:16) and to love the neighbour as myself (Mt. 19:19). I was in a fog of prejudice, half facts and spiritual arrogance. I did not like what I was finding in the privacy of my own heart. As I faced up to the real me, I began to learn the 'rhythms of grace'. I slowly started to feel compassion for the Egyptian Muslims around me who were being required to walk through life's airport unassisted while they could be carried along by the invisible momentum of Jesus' resurrection life. I would hear Muslims refer to God as 'The Merciful and the Compassionate' but their understanding of these grace-related words seemed to be as anaemic as my own understanding of God's grace had been.

I was surprised to find that the absence of grace in Islam is a reason for pride for some Muslims. One imam told me, 'Islam can be summed up in three words – duty, responsibility and discipline.' So to say that Muslims are required to struggle along for God is not a criticism but an observation. Some Muslim scholars define Islam not in terms of submission to the will of God (i.e. passive rest) as we often hear, but as 'striving after righteousness' (i.e. active duty).[9]

I came to suspect that many Muslims are secretly weary of the moral and spiritual burden of trying to please God. A taxi driver in Cairo admitted to me, 'It's easy for you – you're a Christian. It's hard for me – I'm a

Muslim.' He may have meant that Christianity is a western religion that allows more moral freedom and is therefore easier. However, in the course of the conversation, I understood him to be referring to the relentless obligation of Islam, which like Judaism is

> . . . zealous for God . . . but not based on knowledge. Since they did not know the righteousness of God and sought to establish their own, they did not *submit* to God's righteousness. Christ is the end of the law so that there may be righteousness for everyone who believes. (Rom.10:1-4)

Life in the grace of God is *law-free* not *law-less*, but this point would be lost on Muslims such as the weary taxi driver, who was a candidate for the rest on offer from the gentle Christ whose 'burden is light' (Mt. 11:30).

The problem for Muslims is that they cannot be sure whether or not right-standing with God will be attributed to them on Judgement Day. In Islam it all depends on how well they have performed the Five Pillars and Six Beliefs and how God wants to judge them on the day. The good news of right-standing with God by faith without works can therefore be as scandalous to the Muslim mind as it would be to the Jewish mind. Both are likely to react negatively to the Gospel's free gift of right standing with God by faith without the personal honour (*sharaf*) that is earned by self-effort (Eph. 2:8-10).

The performance-orientation in Islam permeates the Muslim society to the point where even people I knew from the Christian minority in Egypt sometimes struggled to maintain a biblical understanding of grace. Human nature naturally defaults to works rather than grace. So it made a big impact on me when I came across Egyptian believers who both grasped grace and lived it out.

The distinctive of grace is expressed well through the following story, which I came across in Egyptian evangelical circles.

A man was walking along a road when he fell into a hole eight feet deep. He broke both arms and both legs and lay there helpless at the bottom of the hole. As he lay there in mortal agony the face of the Buddha appeared at the top of the hole. He looked down at the injured man and began to philosophise about his plight, saying 'You are in a very difficult situation.' The man replied wearily 'I know that but can you help me?' At that the Buddha shook his head and walked away.

Next the face of Muhammad appeared at the top of the hole. Looking down he said 'I too see that you are in a difficult situation. But if you climb half way out till I can reach you, I can pull you out.' The problem was that the man had broken both arms and both legs and was totally helpless. 'But I can't move,' said the man. Muhammad was already walking away.

Lastly Jesus arrived at the top of the hole. He looked down and did not say a word – because he is 'The Word'. He took off his jacket, rolled up his sleeves and climbed down the hole. He picked up the injured man, put him over his shoulder and gave him the 'lift of grace'.

The Christian apologist C. S. Lewis was asked what Christianity's unique feature is among the world religions. 'That's easy,' said Lewis – 'it's grace.' The world religions are DIY systems in which adherents are obliged to resort to self-help. The good news is that the grace of God in Christ is unique because it is the antidote to all self-effort. Yet still the default mechanism kicks in when some earnest Christians try to turn grace back into perfor-mance. To resist that thought is a valid means of 'contending for the faith' (Jude 3). The hymn that captures the essence of grace for me is

> Nothing in my hand I bring,
> Simply to Thy Cross I cling;
> Naked, come to Thee for dress;
> Helpless, look to Thee for grace;
> Foul, I to the fountain fly;
> Wash me, Saviour or I die[10]

When grace confronts human nature it provokes a reaction. Take, for instance, the Apostle Paul who was angrily 'kicking against the goads' (i.e. of grace) (Acts 26:14-16), or the Apostle Peter who attempted to deal with grace by retreating from Jesus' presence – 'Go away from me, Lord; I am a sinful man' (Lk. 5:8).

When I was brought out of local authority care and introduced into the family of my natural father, family members began to be converted around me. Whenever prayer was focused on my unconverted father, he became irritable and difficult to live with and would try to justify himself. The playwright George Bernard Shaw anecdotally reacted to grace with disdain when he said, 'Forgiveness is a mug's game. I'll pay my own debts, thank you.' This is a very Islamic sentiment. As one Muslim said to me, 'I am my own salvation.'

God's grace is only free at the point of our need because it cost God the life of his Son. Neither is God's grace prudently drip-fed to us in accordance with our level of worthiness. It is extravagantly lavished on us, even when we appear to have done our level best to disqualify ourselves from deserving it (1 Jn. 3:1).

I noticed how Jesus modelled grace in his treatment of people such as the woman caught in adultery. He challenged the legalism of her accusers who insisted on implementing the Mosaic Law by stoning her to death. No one asked where the man was who had been involved with the woman in the alleged adultery. This is a comment on the social status of women at the time, which is on a par with their status under Islamic law as practised today. Jesus challenged this mindset by extending grace to the distraught woman with the words – 'Neither do I condemn you.' He then applied the moral lift of grace to her by adding the redemptive rider – 'Go now and leave your life of sin' (Jn. 8:11). I find that divine grace always lifts the recipient.

I realized too that Jesus was teaching grace in his parables. In the story of the labourers in the field, those who had worked all day got the same pay as those who had worked only a fraction of the day (Mt. 20:1-16). Such stories are an intentional reversal of human logic. These parables were carefully orchestrated variations on the grace theme. They were told precisely in order to show that God's grace is not fair in human terms. God's grace is not just amazing – it is downright outrageous.

Naked grace

I came to understand how grace exposes the deepest needs of fallen human beings (Is. 6:5). When grace breaks into our lives it can reduce grown men to blubbering wrecks. This happened in a powerful television reality series called *Monastery*[11] which featured the Benedictine community at Worth Abbey in West Sussex. Five males from a variety of backgrounds and lifestyles agreed to spend 40 days in semi-seclusion with a monk as a spiritual advisor. One of the men, Tony Burke, was a tall handsome blond with the physique of an American footballer. A total spiritual sceptic, Tony worked in the soft porn industry. During the daily celebration of the Eucharist Tony slowly thawed out under the influence of the Holy Spirit, who was exposing the deeper issues in Tony's life where he was in need of the grace of God.

On his last night at the Abbey, Tony has the final consultation with his spiritual advisor. The two men start off as normal but as they proceed they lapse into longer silences as Tony tries to explain what is going on inside him. The viewer is made to feel uncomfortable as Tony's whole demeanour begins to change. He now looks as if he is about to break down. The blond hunk and the grey-haired monk lock eyes. Tony is transfixed by the sympathetic monk who whispers, 'It's OK. Don't try to put it into words – it spoils it.' By now Tony is almost pleading for help as he fights back tears. His moist eyes break away and he looks up at the ceiling to compose himself, then he looks back at the monk.

The room had become the sanctuary of God that Bonhöeffer spoke about.

Eventually the session ends and the monk stands and blesses Tony by laying hands on his bowed head. The monk asks God to make the love within Tony flow into his daily life. I gulped. How can God make his love flow into the soft porn industry? This was naked grace.

Tony left the session like putty in the hands of God. He went out into the night air to have a cigarette and recover. When he was composed enough to speak, he explained to the camera that he had got up that morning a non-believer but was going to bed a believer. He left the monastery and quit his job. He began to make regular visits back to the Abbey in an effort to keep relationships going with the monks. Tony had been marked by grace.

Where to now?

Those early years in Cairo were a foundational time for me. God was building the principles of grace into me first before I could extend grace to Muslims and invite them to share in it. I learned that grace is the place where a Muslim and a Christian can stand together. With this settled in my mind, a whole new vista in Christian living opened up to me. I started to enjoy God's grace for the first time in my own experience. I was changing in relation to grace and was getting ready to move on to investigate how grace relates to Muslims and how I could be the one relating not just with a grace attitude but also with the grace message of Jesus Christ.

The first customer God was to trust me with came across my path sooner than I expected.

Notes

1. Dietrich Bonhöeffer, *The Cost of Discipleship* (New York: Macmillan Publishing Co. Inc., 1963), p45.
2. Jerry Bridges, *Transforming Grace* (Colorado Springs: Nav Press, 1991).
3. David Watson, *Fear No Evil* (London: Hodder and Stoughton, 1984).
4. Henri J. M. Nouwen, *Reaching Out – the Three Movements of the Spiritual Life* (Glasgow: Collins Fount Paperbacks, 1975).
5. *A Dictionary of Christian Theology*, Ed. A Richardson (London: SCM Press Ltd, 1969), p148.
6. *Vine's Expository Dictionary of Biblical Words* (New York: Thomas Nelson Publishers,1985), p100, p277.
   The Hebrew words for grace include *chen* (Deut. 7:7), *hanan* used over eighty times (Gen. 33:5,11; Gen. 43:29; Num. 6:25; Ps. 37:21) and *hen* (Gen. 6:8; 39:21; Ex. 3:21; Ruth 2:10). See page 100. The Greek focuses around the concept of

charis (or grace gift) (Jn. 3:16; 1 Cor. 15:10; 2 Cor. 8:9). See page 277.

The word 'grace' is derived from the Latin *'gratia'* – the basis of 'thank you' in all Latinate languages; for example *'gracias'* in Spanish, *'grazie'* in Italian and *'merci'* in French. Something free is *gratis* and a waiter's tip is a 'gratuity'. A discretionary payment out of kindness is an *ex gratia* payment, most commercial payment periods include twenty-eight days' 'grace' and the British monarchy has it within their power to give 'grace and favour' gifts to their subjects.

7. This paragraph contains the helpful definitions by Dr Joseph Stowell, The Centrality of Christ, in *From Basecamp to Summit*, the Keswick Year Book 2003 (Milton Keynes: Authentic Lifestyle 2003), p13-15.

8. Terry Virgo, *God's Lavish Grace* (Oxford: Monarch, 2004).

9. Ameer Ali, *The Spirit of Islam* (Afro-Asia Publishers, Karachi), 1984, p138.

10. The hymn, Rock of Ages Cleft for Me, Augustus Montague Toplady 1740-78, *Songs of Fellowship* (Eastbourne: Kingsway Music, 1991), No.488, Acts. 26:14-16.

11. *Monastery*, BBC2, TV series of three. Final edition screened on 24 May 2005.

Chapter 3

Grace finds a Muslim

'I can see Jesus in your eyes.'

It was September 1982 and I had just started teaching English in Cairo. A class was dispersing after the lesson in which my students had been improving their spoken English, in order to increase their chances of employment with higher paying foreign companies.

'Do you believe me Mister Steve? – I can see Jesus in your eyes.'

Like 86 per cent of his fellow Egyptians, Ahmad was a Muslim. This had been his first English lesson because he had joined the class a week late – a fairly typical state of affairs for Ahmad when you got to know him for the lovable rascal he was. A student's first attendance usually meant they kept to polite chit-chat rather than in-depth personal conversations, especially with the teacher – but not Ahmad.

By now he had taken hold of my elbow and was steering me to one side as the other students flowed out of the air-conditioned classroom and noisily dispersed into the hot evening air. After a class, even my most able students would revert from their best efforts in English to their native Egyptian dialect of Arabic – the cockney of the Middle East. It is spoken at high speed and with lots of glottal stops, like the distinctive English spoken by Londoners from the East End.

'Excuse me, Ahmad,' I responded. 'What do you mean, you can see Jesus in my eyes?'

I had lowered my voice instinctively because as an expatriate teaching Fellow of the university, there was a tacit understanding that religion and politics (which are the same issue in the Middle East) did not come into the classroom. Proselytising was definitely out of bounds.

I was fairly new to everything and so I was feeling a little uneasy about all sorts of things – not least the direction this conversation with Ahmad was going in. Who was this pushy guy and what did he want?

'I have been watching you and I can see Jesus in your eyes,' he said again in a hushed tone.

He was a stocky young man in his early twenties with short dark brown tightly curled hair and the lemony complexion that is common in the north of Egypt. His face beamed as he spoke about the realization he had just had, in the middle of the English lesson.

'Are you a believer?' I almost whispered as I cleared my throat.

By now it was me who was steering him out of the room into the large noisy thoroughfare outside. This floodlit courtyard was partially shaded during the day by a huge clump of palm trees. It was now just past sunset and the call to prayer crackled from the loudspeakers of a nearby minaret, in this city of a thousand mosques. The *muezzin's* call and the general hubbub of the Cairo traffic made it hard for anyone to overhear us. I began to relax a little.

'Yes – I am a believer,' Ahmad said, looking both ways across my shoulders. His look of pleasure gave me the impression that he had just found out about his own conversion. 'But my new name is Boulos' (Paul), he added. I stepped back and stared at him in amazement. 'Why would he need to change his name?' I asked myself.

'But why are you telling me this, Ahmad?' I prompted him. I was in need of something more to go on. His answer led to a long and involved conversation that lasted through my coffee break until it was time for my next class.

In the early 1980s, conversions such as Ahmad's, although happening occasionally, were rarer than today. Few Muslims were following Jesus and those who did so tended to keep a very low profile. Rarely would one 'out' themselves to a perfect stranger. The fact that Ahmad was telling me this was either an act of crass naïveté on his part or a huge statement of trust, which put a responsibility on me.

Later that evening, Ahmad and I met up again and he began to tell me his story. We strolled around the campus in the dark and eventually went to the cafeteria for some coffee. We took it outside and sipped at a wicker table painted red under the palms.

Ahmad was born near Alexandria on the north coast. He was one of eight children. His parents had moved to the capital, like so many others from around the country, in search of a better life. This drift to the big city often led to a similar standard of living as before – if not worse. These families left their home in a sea of provincial poverty to settle in Cairo where they found themselves in an ocean of poverty. Like many other families, Ahmad's lived in the middle of an endless urban sprawl. Family harmony became essential in such cramped quarters and Ahmad's family usually managed quite well but Ahmad occasionally did not get on with the elder of his two brothers and he never got on well with his father who, like Ahmad, was a warm but stubborn man with a fiery temper.

Ahmad's encounter with Jesus Christ was linked to his general drive to improve himself. He began listening to a European Christian radio station that he picked up on his small shortwave radio. This was one benefit of living so high up in a building that frequently had no electricity – let alone a lift. The broadcasts caught his attention because they were in English. He had been tuning in twice a week for over a year by the time we met. As far as he was concerned, it was a free English lesson in which he would try to understand as much as he could while furiously scribbling down any new words or phrases he heard. One day he discovered that an Arabic programme followed the English one. He began to leave the radio on to listen in Arabic when family members were out.

Ahmad's attention slowly shifted from the language to the content of the programmes. He started to use the English programme for its language content and the Arabic for its spiritual content. To help him follow what was being said, Ahmad bought the smallest Arabic Bible he could find from a Christian bookshop, where he pretended to be from the Christian Orthodox community. This stopped the owners feeling nervous about serving a Muslim, which some might have challenged as illegal. The first thing Ahmad did was to disguise the Bible by covering it in newspaper – a common thing for Egyptian students to do with a study book.

Armed with his new Bible, Ahmad embarked on the second phase of his encounter with Christ. He wrote to the address given on the radio programme to enrol in a Bible correspondence course. He had this sent to a friend's post box at a government post office some distance from his home.

As the months rolled on, it was not so much Ahmad's Islamic values or beliefs that were changing but the way he perceived God – and himself in relation to God. Ahmad's perception of God had been of a lofty unknowable Being who did not need or want any relationship with mortals. When Ahmad 'did' his Islamic prayers, he said it was as though God was listening from a distance. As he learned about the Bible account of God it challenged this picture; for example in the Garden of Eden God calls out for Adam (Gen. 3:8-9). Ahmad was intrigued by the biblical assertion that God can be known and wants to be known by humankind. Which contrasted with Islam's teaching that God cannot be known and does not want relationship with humans.

Ahmad respected Islam's prophet Muhammad as a spiritual authority figure as well as a military leader but he began to feel strangely drawn towards Jesus Christ in the Qur'an; for example where Christ is mentioned in Sura 3 verses 45-55.

Behold, the angel said: 'O Mary, Allah giveth thee glad tidings of a Word from Him: his name will be Jesus Christ, the son of Mary, held in honour in this world and the hereafter' . . .

She said: 'O my Lord. How shall I have a son when no man hath touched me?'

He said: 'Even so: Allah createth what He willeth . . . And Allah will teach him the Book and Wisdom, the Law and the Gospel and appoint him a Messenger . . . with this message: 'I have come to you, with a Sign from your Lord . . . and I heal those born blind, and the lepers and I quicken the dead, by Allah's leave' . . .

Behold, Allah said: 'O Jesus. I will take thee and raise thee to Myself . . . I will make those who follow thee superior to those who reject faith, to the Day of Resurrection.'

Ahmad followed such passages up by reading the full account of Jesus' life in the *injîl* (New Testament). Jesus' heart seemed to beat in a way that contrasted with the Islamic theme of power. He noticed how Jesus 'made himself nothing', 'took on himself the form of a servant', 'humbled himself' (Phil. 2:7-8), reached out to the marginalized, championed the weak and sided with the vulnerable and sick. The New Testament expression 'the *grace* of our Lord Jesus Christ' (2 Cor. 8:9) started to have real meaning for Ahmad.

The radio programmes and the correspondence course began to reveal Jesus as the consistent theme throughout the Bible. Ahmad found that Jesus was the one who was foretold by the prophets[1] and that when Jesus was born, he caused supernatural activity in the stars (Mt. 2:9-10) and was referred to as 'God with us' (Is. 7:14). The Apostle Paul described Jesus as being the one through whom and for whom everything in the cosmos was created and that he was the visible representation of the invisible God, with the fullness of Deity residing in him (Col. 1:15-16; 2:9, 10b). Ahmad became enthralled as he realized that Jesus must be more than a prophet. I remember his insistence 'He is more. He is more.'

By this point in his pilgrimage Ahmad felt that the choice was less between Muhammad and Christ and more about rendering to Muhammad the things that were his and to Christ the things which were his. Although a controversial thought for us western Christians, ultimately even the prophet Muhammad and the Qur'an became stepping-stones facilitating Ahmed's journey to Christ. It had become clear to him that Jesus' moral and spiritual authority was total and that what he demanded from Ahmad was not some new external observance alongside his Islam but the redirecting of it. Ahmad had never practised this level of 'submission' to God in all his years growing up in his Muslim family. He had never been devout, although he did regularly practise the parts of Islam that he chose to observe, such as eating *halal* food, avoiding alcohol, 'doing' the Friday prayers (rather than praying five times a day) and keeping the Ramadan fast.

Meanwhile Ahmad kept up his link over the airwaves with the voices of the radio presenters. He gradually trusted the Christ he had always been vaguely aware of as a revered prophet in Islam. Ahmad never said the conventional evangelical 'Sinner's Prayer', instead he heard the Good News about Jesus by radio, looked into the claims in the Bible, found that (to the best of his understanding) Jesus was more than a prophet and was totally trustworthy and simply started to talk to him and follow his teaching within his Muslim context. What mattered was that Ahmad was enjoying the life of Christ.

All was well until Ahmad's father discovered him reading the Bible. In the heated discussion that followed Ahmad blurted out that he had 'become a Christian'. This provoked an all-out family row during which Ahmad lost his temper and his father became so furious that he beat him quite badly. Ahmad said that with hindsight he realized his father was hurt by what he might be getting himself into. He had lashed out in desperation, driven by the shame it would bring on the family if the news reached the wider community. There would also be legal problems if anyone reported it to the authorities. Matters got daily worse to the point that his mother never stopped crying and Ahmad knew he could only keep the peace by moving out – temporarily at least. He managed to find a tiny bed-sit in another district where he soon learned that other male relatives had threatened to kill him in order to regain the family honour. This meant a separation of several months until everyone had calmed down.

Sadly his problems got worse. Ahmad was looking for other 'followers' like himself but he found no one. He then tried Coptic Christians who were usually identifiable by their distinctive names and the Jerusalem cross they had tattooed in blue on one of their wrists. Each time Ahmad approached someone and said what he was, he was politely rebuffed. This happened several times until he gave up. Either they did not understand such a spiritual re-orientation or they did not believe he was genuine. When he did find someone who believed him, they were too afraid to get involved – just in case of problems. He understood the difficulty he faced as a Muslim following Jesus but he had not anticipated the extent of the difficulty that this would cause cultural Christians. He did not appreciate just how high the stakes were for the Christian community too.

Ahmad continued to listen to the radio and wait. Eventually he found himself sitting in my English class. In the middle of the lesson something had clearly told him that 'Mister Steve' (as my students called me) was a western follower of Jesus and therefore freer of the local sensitivities and that he would be able to believe him and help him. Ahmad needed not so much a 'spiritual midwife' as a Barnabas who could provide 'spiritual friendship';[2] someone who would be prepared to walk and talk with him as he re-oriented his life towards Jesus Christ.

I never did get to the bottom of why Ahmad had used the expression 'become a Christian' to his father. If only he had said that he was 'following the prophet Jesus'. It seemed that he had picked up this expression from the radio programme without realizing the explosion it would cause. Now it was too late to take the words back. To the family, Ahmad had betrayed everything he stood for – his religion, his family, his culture and even his country. I felt the whole situation was so unfortunate and sad. I did not yet know enough to appreciate that this degree of conflict was not necessary and that there were other ways to follow Jesus in an Islamic context. I knew that Ahmad could be a headstrong person and that family rows were not new, though this one was clearly very serious. He continued to go to work, listen to his radio and to follow his correspondence course while waiting for whatever would happen next.

I knew that I must be careful how I got involved. They say that if a chrysalis is helped to hatch into a butterfly it may never fly properly. Apparently the struggle is a necessary part of strengthening the wings to make survival possible. So too with followers of Jesus from Muslim backgrounds like Ahmad. I learned when it was best not to interfere and just be supportive.

As I drew alongside him, I probably felt more vulnerable than Ahmad did but we managed to become 'spiritual friends'. I was a westerner who did not really understand fully what Ahmad was facing but I was prepared to work at it. We were both trying to figure out how to follow Jesus in a new environment. For me, it was as a western follower of Jesus in my newly adopted Egyptian culture and for Ahmad, it was his new-found counter-cultural faith in Christ. We continued to meet over coffee in my breaks and then later on we added some evening meetings when there was no English class for either of us. We lived at opposite ends of Cairo so to meet in the middle at the university was good for us both. It was some months before we could sort out some more permanent fellowship for Ahmad. Until that point our coffee dates became his only 'church'. I knew this arrangement was acceptable to the Christ who said 'Where (even) two or three come together in my name I am with them' (Mt. 18:20).

Ahmad eventually made an uneasy truce with his father but remained separated from his family. He was only the first of several followers of Jesus from Muslim backgrounds that I was to meet in Egypt. Our relationship was to prove a turning point for me, which led to an adventure in which I was to take the message of God's love for Muslims to Christians and the implications of the Muslim presence in the West to politicians and journalists around the world.

What started in that classroom on a warm night in 1982 was just the beginning.

Notes

1. Isaiah 9:1-7; 11:1-14; Micah 5:2.
2. Brian McLaren, *More Ready than You Realize – evangelism as dance in the post-modern matrix* (Grand Rapids: Zondervan, 2002), p23.

Grace for the dark side?

'He will be a wild donkey of a man; his hand will be
against everyone and everyone's hand will be against him,
and he will live in hostility towards all his brothers.'
(Gen. 16:12)

Out of the blue, an email from the USA arrived. It was from
an American Christian I did not know. He described how
he had prayed the night before with Hamid (name
changed), an Iraqi Kurd. The young man had started to
follow Jesus but had no Arabic Bible; he knew no other
believers and was due to return to Kurdistan in days and
could I help? I got onto my contacts in Hamid's home
town. They met him soon after he arrived back, supplied a
Bible and were ready to help him carefully integrate into
the local network of the followers of Jesus. Within two
weeks the American contact copied to me an email he had
received from Hamid's best friend. It described, in broken
English, how Hamid had been gunned down in the street
in broad daylight – 'for his faith in Christ'. You can imagine
my distress and sense of guilt for helping a new brother in
Christ to go to his death; an unsuspecting martyr.

On another occasion I was sent details of a Christian website that was worse than pornography. It contained a collection of viewable video clips of Islamists who were inspired by, if not linked with, Al-Qaeda. The clips showed these men sawing off the heads of their victims and then holding them up for the camera. I watched three such executions before I felt too physically ill to continue. I confess that I struggle with feelings of hatred for such people.

I am angry with such Muslims who are engaged in 'politicized Islam'. They press for political change in Islam's favour by the brutalization of non-Muslims through a variety of means that include sheer violence but also those that are peaceful, diplomatic, academic and even cultural. Militant Islam clearly has a case to answer in the twenty-first century.

The dark side of Islam came crashing into American life on 11 September 2001 and then into the daily life of Britain in the London Transport attacks on 7 July 2005. The 'Islamikaze' atrocities had a comparable effect in Britain as the attacks on America did. The British reaction may have been characteristically stoical and more subdued but in both cases there was a sense of public confidence before the event and one of nervous unease and defiance after it.

Those I am calling 'ordinary' Muslims also suffered as a result of the London attacks: directly as victims and indirectly through the racist backlash against them. Acid was poured over the car of a Muslim neighbour of a friend of mine three days after 7/7. I was invited to a briefing of community leaders by the Chief Constable of the West Midlands Police Force where we were told that a Muslim woman had her car rammed. After this, the male driver got out, spat at her and verbally abused her.

The significance of the London Transport bombings was that not only had an Al-Qaeda-inspired cell struck in

Britain but the bombers were British-born. They were not only *jihadi* fundamentalists, but also (unlike the bombings in Casablanca, Istanbul and Madrid before it) *takfiri*s: the 'anti-infidel' fighters who are intent on suicide as a way of martyrdom. These are not 'ordinary' Muslims.

The London bombings led to unprecedented public denunciations of Islamic terrorism by Muslim leaders. Yet the uncomfortable reality dawned on us all, that while all Muslims were not terrorists, all such terrorists have identified themselves as Muslims. This has challenged Muslims to account for the lunatic fringe who say they are acting in the name of Islam, which the moderates claim is a religion of peace. Expediency forces politicians and Islamic leaders to attempt to distance Islam from the atrocities. The Mayor of London Ken Livingstone claimed in a rally in Trafalgar Square that the attacks were by people of 'no belief at all'. This was an unconvincing attempt to account for the violence in the name of Islam. The under-reported fact of the matter is that the Qur'an itself contains over a hundred violent *jihadic* passages and a hundred and nine passages urging war in the name of Islam.[1] This was carefully avoided in an effort to dissociate Islam from violence – a point that could have fuelled ultra right wing groups such as the British National Party. If it were more widely known by the general public, it could have sparked serious community friction.

Journalist Charles Moore wrote a perceptive piece in response to the London bombings noting the total absence of a 'Gandhi figure in Islam'. Moore asserted that it was an extreme interpretation of Islam that threatened Britain, based on a literal doctrine that, unlike modern expressions of Christianity, was 'politically and militarily oriented'. He added that it seemed reasonable to 'ask

Muslims what the violent passages of the Qur'an mean in the modern world'.[2]

Christians need to recognize that, while the Gospel mandate is to *reach* the world with a message (as opposed to Islam's mandate to *subjugate* it), there are violent passages in the Old Testament which also need careful explanation; such as the slaughter of the people of Shechem (Gen. 34); the violent execution of Achan and his entire family (Josh. 7); the violent destruction of Ai (Josh. 8:1-39); bloody civil war in Israel (Judg. 20); Samuel's command for the slaughter of Amalekite men, women, children and livestock (1 Sam. 15:1-5) and the seizure of infants to smash them against rocks (Ps. 137:9).

The Bible has been used by some Dutch Reformed churches in South Africa to support apartheid and by some American Christian fundamentalists who feel justified in bombing abortion clinics in the name of Christ.

In the course of my work I am obliged to look carefully at Islam's darker side more than most westerners. So I am well aware of the fact that a debate is going on within Muslim circles about how to interpret the overtly violent passages in the Qur'an; how to decide which verses are akin to the western 'Just War' principle; and how to understand the Qur'anic passages which espouse the limitation of violence in the pursuit of justice; for example, 'Bear witness to the truth in all equity; and never let hatred of anyone lead you into deviating from justice' (S5.8); 'Repel evil with that which is better' (S23.96); 'Do not take any human being's life which God hath declared to be sacred – other than in the pursuit of justice' (S6.51).

Politicized Islam is driven by the core concept of *jihâd*, which is an Arabic word meaning to 'strive' morally, spiritually and (where necessary) violently in the way of

God. The *jihadic* theme is extensive in the Qur'an,[3] which makes it easy for both radical Muslims and their critics to claim that it is the primary theme of Islam. This is an embarrassment to fair-minded Muslims who realize that the holy book of Islam raises these difficult issues. Like some fundamentalist streams in Christianity, many Muslims are taught to interpret the Qur'an literally. Traditional Islamic scholarship does not allow new ways of applying the Qur'an in the modern world. This is reflected in the 1928 motto of the first Muslim Brotherhood (*ikhwân al-muslimun*), which was founded in Egypt by Hasan al-Banna. Their motto was 'Allah is our objective. The Prophet is our leader. The Qur'an is our law. Jihad is our way. Dying in the way of Allah is our highest hope.'[4]

The confusion for Muslims and westerners about the nature of Islam starts with the Arabic word *islâm*. This means 'submission' but with the connotation of 'submissive peace' i.e. peace only through submission to God. This works in three ways; firstly a personal relationship to God by submissive obedience to him; secondly the duty to actively ensure the submission of others in the extended family, wider clan and the *umma* at large; thirdly the imperative of Islamic *da'wa* (mission) to bring the non-Muslim (*kâfir*) to Islam. So to say, as many non-Arabic speaking Muslims do, that Islam means peace is not strictly accurate.

Muslims are faced with the decision of whether the literal interpretation of the Qur'an subverts it or is faithful to it. While militancy is proving divisive among the majority of moderate Muslims, some Muslims are becoming disillusioned with the militant agenda and are as concerned as many westerners about how relentless it is in its aggression towards non-Muslims all over the world. Political analyst Samuel P. Huntington pointed out the existence of violence that, he says,

... occurs between Muslims on the one hand, and against the Orthodox Serbs in the Balkans on the other. Violence has gone on against Jews in Israel, against the Hindus in India, against the Buddhists in Burma and Catholics in the Philippines. Islam has bloody borders.[5]

The violent Islamist agenda is nourished by the previous thinking of men like Abul 'Ala Mawdudi, the founder of the radical Pakistani Muslim brotherhood *Jamat-i-Islami*, who said

Islam is a revolutionary faith that comes to destroy any government made by man ... The goal of Islam is to rule the entire world. Any nation that tries to get in the way of that goal, Islam will fight and destroy ... Islam is a one-way door, you can enter through it but you cannot leave.[6]

This is pure totalitarianism, something that the Muslim brotherhoods have always been in danger of. However, it is also fair to say that these groups can be driven by understandable political objectives, which have varied over the decades according to the political landscape. For example, while the early groups focused on ridding the Middle East of western cultural influences in education and the law, Al-Qaeda focus on issues such as the secularism of western society, western 'interference' in Muslim lands such as Iraq and the West's inaction over Palestine.

In May 2004, *Time* magazine described the videotaped beheading of American technician, Daniel Pearl, in Karachi, Pakistan. The gruesome video included a message from the late Abu Musab Al-Zarqawi, who was the third most wanted Al-Qaeda operative. Al-Zarqawi claimed that the execution was sanctioned by the Qur'an as follows – 'When you meet the Unbelievers (i.e. in

jihadic fight) smite their necks' (S47.4). The same Arabic
expression for 'strike the neck' is rendered in colloquial
Egyptian Arabic as 'break the neck'. I have often heard
this expression used as a threat in Middle Eastern street
fights. Abu Musab al-Zarqawi went on to ask, 'Has the
time not come for you to lift the sword, which the master
of the Messengers (i.e. Muhammad) was sent with? The
Prophet ordered (Muslims) to cut off the heads of some of
the prisoners of (the Battle of) Badr. He is our example.'[7]

The *Time* article also referred to the *The New York Times*
report on the beheading of the Egyptian Muslim,
Muhammad Fawzi. He had allegedly collaborated with the
Americans in Iraq. A member of the anti-American
insurgence fighters stood over Fawzi quoting the words of
the Qur'an – 'He who will abide by the Qur'an will
prosper; he who offends against it will get the sword.' Then
two men forced Fawzi to the ground and severed his head.

The article in *The New York Times* went on to attempt a
balance to this horror by quoting Sheikh Khaled Abou El-
Fadl, professor of Islamic Law at UCLA, who claimed that
the understanding of the Qur'an that drives Al-Qaeda was
'discounted long ago'. His reading of the situation in Iraq
was that religious study had been discouraged for thirty
years under Saddam Hussein and that this has led to
ignorance among younger members of the insurgence
who are trying to educate themselves in Islam as they go
along. This, according to Professor El-Fadl, makes them
vulnerable to the manipulation of teachers such as Abu
Musab Al-Zarqawi. Such a rationalization would be more
significant if it came from leaders within the Muslim
world. The real theological authority in Islam lies with its
clerics and not with academics who happen to be
Muslims. Such people adopt the apologetic position
within western universities where they have less influence
on Muslims.

The heroes of the London bombers had been *mujahideen* in Kosovo or Afghanistan or else those they regard as spiritual authorities, such as Osama bin Laden.

Liberal Muslim activist and writer Irshad Manji joins the call for Muslims to stop being 'in denial' about the fact that it is the Qur'an that endorses such violence. She says

> Sir Iqbal Sacranie, secretary-general for the Muslim Council of Britain, is an example (i.e. of a prominent moderate Muslim who is ignored by the young radicals). He listed what he saw as the potential incentives to bomb innocent people, including 'alienation' and 'segregation.' But Islam? God forbid that the possibility even be entertained. That is the dangerous denial from which mainstream Muslims need to emerge. For too long, we Muslims have been sticking fingers in our ears and chanting 'Islam means peace' to drown out the negative noise from our holy book. Far better to own up to it, not erase or revise it, just recognize it and thereby join moderate Jews and Christians in confessing the 'sins of Scripture.' In doing so, Muslims would show a thoughtful side that builds trust with the wider communities of the West.[8]

It is not surprising that western Christians are as biased as non-Christians against Muslims because they are only presented by media images of Muslims linked to kidnappings, suicide bombings, beheadings or siege situations such as at the Beslan school in Russia. Prominent media Muslims include militants such as Abu-Hamza Al-Masri the hook-handed former imam of the Finnesbury Park mosque, and the militant Islamic celebrity Omar Bakri Muhammad, the leader in Britain of Hizb ut-Tahrir (Party of Liberation). He put his arm around the shoulder of a colleague of mine who is a Christian debater with

Muslims, and smiled as he told a group of Muslims, 'This is my friend and when the Islamic *khalifa* [rule] is declared in the UK, he will be the first one that I kill.' Thankfully, Muslims like him are a minority. Arrogant men such as Omar Bakri give westerners all the ammunition they need to resent all Muslims.

I was in London on business just after the July 2005 bombings. As I got out of my taxi a businessman rushed out of a restaurant and grabbed a laptop off the shoulder of a smart but casually dressed olive-skinned man. Apparently the olive-skinned man had just stolen the laptop from the businessman and walked out of the restaurant. The taxi driver said, 'It's those ******* Arabs again.' After twenty-five years as a Middle Eastern analyst I can usually spot an Arab when I see one – the thief was no Arab. I continued my journey into Paddington Station and used the public conveniences before boarding my train. On the wall was scrawled 'Don't give in to the Muslim *****.'

The next day a suspected suicide-bomber was chased into the London underground and shot dead by police. All eye-witnesses identified the dead man as a Pakistani. He turned out to be twenty-seven-year-old Jean Charles de Menezes – a Brazilian who was totally innocent. It is sad that recent events have influenced the British public to assume that anyone who is not a white Caucasian is suspect.

This negative stereotyping of Muslims is strengthened by TV programmes such as the BBC2 documentary *Don't Panic I'm Islamic*[9] in which a broad cross-section of British Muslims were shown expressing anger about western intervention in Iraq, the perceived economic and cultural domination of Muslim lands, the West's double standards over the Palestinian situation and the refusal to require Israel to implement UN resolutions that other countries are invaded for ignoring. Articulate young Muslims are noticing that the West has the political will to go where it is not wanted in the Muslim world, while suffering from a lack of political will to intervene in the Palestinian situation where their involvement would be welcomed by most Muslims.

One Muslim academic agreed with me privately that Islamic tradition 'suffers from an inability to be self-critical'. Perhaps this explains why there is such sensitivity on the part of Muslims when westerners try to be as objective about the past failures of Muslims as they have been about the failures within Christendom. Having acknowledged the failures of Christendom such as the oppressive domination of church over state in the Spanish Inquisition, western aggression in the name of God against Muslims and the regrettable aspects of the colonial era where the distinction between Christianity and commerce became blurred. Some non-Muslims are still asking such questions as:

- Why is Islam unable to critique itself?
- Why is Islam so resistant to change?
- Why do Muslim countries suffer from such poor human rights records?
- Why has the enforcing of Shari'a law caused bloodshed, chaos and/or economic ruin wherever it has been attempted e.g. Afghanistan, Iran, Nigeria, Sudan and Pakistan?
- Why is it left to Christian aid agencies to help Muslims in times of famine and natural disaster?
- Why are the majority of asylum seekers fleeing from Islamic states?
- Why do Islamic oil states use their wealth freely to propagate Islam while doing little to alleviate poverty among their own citizens, let alone in Africa?
- Why have fifteen million Muslims come as economic migrants to the 'infidel' lands of Europe?[10]

I believe God is calling western Christians to be aware of the past downside to Christianity and Islam and choose a grace response towards Muslims.

Why are we so negative about ordinary Muslims? If rain is forecast in Britain, we instinctively see its negative impact on what we want to do that day. When my wife Julia and I lived in a rural community, we began to understand the positives that rain brings. Rain enriches the agricultural life of Britain and makes food possible. It is the same with the Muslim presence in the West; western Christians tend to see the proverbial glass as half empty rather than half full. It is always easier to focus on the negatives and miss the positives that Muslims contribute to western life. We will identify some of these later.

The negative attitude of many Christians towards Muslims is partly due to the over-romanticizing of the Holy Land that has come about through the idealized teaching of biblical history and biblical prophecy. This can lead to the blurring of the distinction between 'prophetic Israel' and the current reality of the political State of Israel. We must remember that there is also considerable Jew/Jew conflict over what some claim to be anti-biblical government policies. It has been rightly said that as far as the Holy Land is concerned 'it is easy to get caught up in the book of Revelation, rather than to live out the Sermon on the Mount'.[11] There is a brand of biblical eschatology that can lead to the conclusion that Palestinian Muslims (and all other Muslims by default) are the enemy because they are seen as working against biblical prophecy. In reality, a significant number of Palestinians are Orthodox Christians.

The Israeli/Palestinian conflict is more about justice than Islam. It is the Islamic faith of Palestinian Muslims that has sustained them during, what they see as, a struggle against human rights abuses. Sadly, the ideology of Islam has become the vehicle for fanatical Palestinian Muslims to inflict equal human rights abuses on Jews in the spiralling 'tit-for-tat' confrontation from which all sides, including some western powers, need to repent.

Christian negativity towards Muslims is also rooted in the demonising phraseology used by some people when referring to them. I have heard Christians refer to Muslims as the 'Satanic menace', the 'anti-Christ' and the 'forces of darkness' arrayed against Israel. The logical conclusion to these terms is that the average Muslim must be demonised in some way. When I unpack this sort of statement I find that it is sometimes a reaction to cultural differences and (for the westerner) the strangeness of Muslim culture. It is rarely about the Christian discerning any actual demonization of the Muslim.

Christian negativity may also be based on watching so many inner-cities become dominated by Asians. This 'inner-city invasion', as one Birmingham lady put it to me, refers to the feelings of local white people who have witnessed what they see as the displacement of the Christian presence by Muslims. In reality the Muslim ghettos came about through a process in which many indigenous white people grew more affluent, and moved out of the inner-cities to the more expensive housing in the suburbs, leaving the cheaper housing for the Muslims (particularly Asians) to move into. Close-knit Asian families drew in other extended family members and the process was complete – a predominantly white area became predominantly Asian. For example, St Philip's Anglican church in Leicester saw its electoral roll shrink from 900 to 49 over a twenty-five year period.[12]

Another reason for Christian negativity towards Muslims could be the visits of some overseas mission workers to supporting churches. Their sincere concern about the 'challenge' of Islam can convey the subliminal message that the Gospel cannot penetrate Islamic countries. I have heard some missionary 'horror stories' told to congregations in an effort to inspire prayer and financial support. This approach can accidentally have the opposite effect. Only 2 per cent of global mission resources are invested in direct mission to the 1.2 billion Muslims who make up a fifth of the globe. There is one Christian worker for every one million Muslims. One minister said to me, 'Let's just do what we do best and concentrate on indigenous white people.' Another said, 'We invest in the areas where we know we will get some sort of result.' Few in the western church seem to believe that Muslims will be saved.

Christians have understandably reacted to the fact that 169,000 Christians were martyred in 2004, mainly in Muslim countries.[13] The journalist Anthony Browne reports that an estimated three million Christians are either threatened with violence or legally discriminated against because of their faith.

> Across the Islamic world, Christians are being persecuted. Saudi Arabia bans churches, public Christian worship, the Bible and the sale of Christmas cards, and stops non-Muslims from entering Mecca. Christians are regularly imprisoned and tortured on trumped-up charges of drinking, insulting Islam or Bible-bashing.[14]

When it was the Communist regimes that were known to be responsible for persecution and death, we managed to separate out the individuals from the system they lived under; not so with Muslims who become the personification of the atrocities.

The Islamic scene is clearly a mixture of both light and darkness. Anyone who attempts to balance such opposites is going to feel conflict and is likely to be misunderstood by both Christians and Muslims. I have found this exercise costly. One imam asked me, 'Who are you leaving behind on your side in order to do what you are doing?' I was sad to admit that I have left quite a few Christian friends behind to become a peacemaker (Mt. 5:9). Some Muslims dislike it when I encourage Christians to discuss the good news about Jesus with ordinary Muslims but then some Christians do not like me having the 'affection of Christ' for Muslims either (Phil. 1:8).

It is not easy to urge a grace response when people feel threatened. This is the real challenge. After the London Transport bombings the offices of the Muslim Council of Britain reported that their office had received several thousand aggressive emails calling for 'war on Muslims throughout Britain'.[15] While Sir Iqbal Sacranie, Chairman of the Council, was filming an interview for BBC1 news he was jostled and slapped in the face by young Muslim men for publicly denouncing extremism. I can relate to Sir Iqbal, who stands between two camps within the Muslim community. I, too, have been accused by Christians of being either politically naïve, theologically liberal, or both. However, the grace-response is a stance that Jesus Christ demanded of his followers when he commanded them to 'love your enemies and pray for those who persecute you' (Mt. 5:44). The Apostle Paul also urged, 'Bless those who persecute you; bless and do not curse.' Likewise his response to suffering Christians was to 'mourn with those who mourn'. His response to those who do damage to the Body of Christ was, 'Do not repay anyone evil for evil . . . Do not take revenge' (Rom. 12:14-21).

One of the most powerful and moving examples of how grace wipes up the mess made by the ugly bigotry of others occurred in another setting, where you were either white and acceptable or other race and unacceptable.

This issue was addressed in the South African Truth and Reconciliation process.

> During the days of the Truth and Reconciliation Commission, a frail 70-year-old black woman stands slowly to her feet. Facing her across the courtroom are several white police officers, one of whom, Mr. Van der Broek, has just been found guilty of the murders of both the woman's son and her husband some years before. Van der Broek had come to the woman's home, taken her son, shot him at point-blank range and then burned the young man's body on a fire while he and his officers partied nearby.

> Several years later, Van der Broek and his cohorts had returned to take away her husband as well. For many months she heard nothing of her husband's whereabouts. Then, almost two years after his disappearance, Van der Broek came back to get the old woman herself. How vividly she remembers that evening, going down to a place beside a river where she was shown her husband, bound and beaten, but still strong in spirit, lying on a pile of wood. The last words she heard from his lips as the officers poured gasoline over his body and set him aflame were 'Father, forgive them.'

> And now the woman stands in the Courtroom and listens to the confessions offered by Mr. Van der Broek. A member of the Truth and Reconciliation Commission turns to her and asks, 'So, what do you want? How should justice be done to this man who has destroyed your family?'

> 'I want three things', begins the old woman calmly. 'I want first to be taken to the place where my husband's body was burned so that I can gather up the dust and give his remains a decent burial.'

> She pauses, then continues. 'My husband and son were my only family, so I want, secondly, for Mr. Van der Broek to become my son. I want him to come twice a month to the

ghetto and spend a day with me so I can pour on him whatever love I still have left in me.

'And finally', she says, 'I want a third thing. I would like Mr. Van der Broek to know that I offer him my forgiveness because Jesus Christ died so we could be forgiven. This was also the wish of my husband. And so, I ask for someone to come to my side and help me across this Courtroom so I can take Mr. Van der Broek in my arms, embrace him and let him know that he is truly forgiven.'

As the court assistants come to lead the old woman across the Courtroom, Mr. van der Broek, overwhelmed by what he has just heard, faints. As he does, those in the courtroom – friends, family, neighbours – all victims of decades of oppression and injustice, begin to sing, softly, but with assurance . . .

'Amazing Grace, how sweet the sound that saved a wretch like me. I once was lost but now I'm found, was blind but now I see'.[16]

A Christian minister once asked what kept me going in my commitment to serve Muslims. This is usually an easy question, except for the fact that it was asked in the presence of two bearded Iranian Shi'ite clerics. The difficulty was trying to explain myself to both Christian and Muslim at the same time. I was pinned down in no-man's-land. As I searched for the right words, I could feel myself becoming emotional. I caught the eye of one of the Iranian clerics and said: 'It's a sense of compulsion by the love of Christ for you that keeps me going' (2 Cor. 5:14). The Muslims looked puzzled and uncomfortable.

I realize that responding with grace is a high ideal, as are all of Jesus' commandments. I am not pretending that there is no danger of us becoming naïve. However, it is clear: grace towards the Muslim is possible. This is because it is under-girded by the biblical certainty that the divine plan will win out. Of course, this is not easy to say to Christians such as those in the north of Nigeria who asked me what they should do after they have already 'turned the other cheek' several times. Politically motivated Muslim leaders stir up unemployed and impressionable young Muslims with a bad attitude to agree to be bussed into neighbouring townships to burn churches and kill Christians. This kind of funda-mentalism is the misguided use of the ideology of Islam to achieve a political goal of a united Nigeria under Islam. These campaigns for political domination usually have a tribal dimension in Africa where your tribe and your religion tend to be the same. The ongoing plight of African and Asian followers of Jesus under this sort of pressure helps put the intimidation we feel in Europe into a more manageable perspective. I am reassured by the biblical bottom line that it is God who is steering human history, politicized Islam included, to his appointed end (Eph. 1:11).

I have already mentioned that St Francis of Assisi was a positive role model of grace towards Muslims. Most people know him to be the saintly monk who was pictured with birds sitting on his shoulder while he talked to the animals – a kind of mediaeval Dr Doolittle. However, St Francis should be remembered as a true icon of Christian grace towards Muslims at a time when Christian/Muslim relations were, in some respects, worse than today. During his lifetime in the thirteenth century, the West and Islam were locked into negative stereotyping and political animosity that broke out into periodic violence and the land-grabbing that triggered the Crusades. Francis sent out monks of his own Order to wage a war of prayer, powerlessness, poverty and recon-ciliation. This was a contrast to the Muslim Ottoman armies and the Crusader spirit. St. Francis the apostle of grace was a modest mystic who was artistic, depressive and eccentric: a humble man who was said to have died singing. He preached to Muslim and European soldiers in France and Spain and even spent time in Egypt, where he had a life-changing encounter with the Muslim commander, Sultan Al-Kamil, who was profoundly influenced for Christ.

Francis instructed his monks not to preach until they had demonstrated the Gospel of love, peace and reconciliation for a lengthy period; 'Wherever you go,' he said, 'share the Gospel – sometimes with words.'[17] When people ask me what my approach to Muslims is, if I am thinking quickly enough I tend to say that different Muslims need different approaches from Christians of different temperaments. However, the approach that suits me best is the Franciscan approach. I have been enriched through the Old Testament aspects of Muslim life and practice which have survived over fourteen hundred years. However, I have also been beaten, spat at, threatened with weapons, used, lied to and put out of the country by the Secret Police. But like St Francis, I have discovered how to move beyond *grievance* against Muslims and towards *grace* for them.

Notes

1. Don Richardson, *The Real message of the Koran* (California: Regal Venture, 2003), Appendix B, p254.
2. Charles Moore, News Review – 'Where is the Gandhi of Islam?' (*Daily Telegraph,* Saturday 9 July 2005), p19.
3. See for example the Qur'an Sura 2.190; 4.89; 5.51; 9.5,14,38,41,123 and 60.1.
   The word *jihâd* is an Arabic term that means to 'strive' or 'struggle' in the way of Islam. This means the effort to

perform Islam properly starting with the five pillars and including family and civil duties. However, when Islamic interests are threatened or damaged it is permitted to engage in military *jihâd* or what westerners call 'holy war'. From *jihâd* come other words such as *jihâdi* and *mujâhideen* (i.e. Islamic fighters in military *jihâd* in the singular and plural forms of the word).

4. Source: Internet article by Lorenzo Vidino, 'The Muslim Brotherhood's Conquest of Europe'.

5. Samuel P. Huntington, *The Clash of Civilisations and the Remaking of World Order* (Carmichael, California: Touchstone Books, 1998).

6. Mawlâna Abul 'Ala Mawdûdi, *Jihad in Islam*, India: 1970, cited in *Islam and Terrorism*, M. Gabriel (Lake Mary Florida: Charisma Books, 2002), p82. *Murtaddki Sâza Islâmi Qâwmi Mein*, Islamic Publications (Lahore: 8th Edn., 1981).

7. David Van Biema, 'Does the Koran condone killing?' (*Time* magazine, 20 September, 2004).

8. Irshad Manji, 'When denial can kill' (*Time* magazine, Sunday 17 July 2005).

9. BBC2, *Don't Panic I'm Islamic*, 12 June 2005.

10. Clifford Hill, 'Opening Up Islam' (*Prophecy Today*: Jan/Feb 2002), p4-5.

11. Hazel Southam, 'A challenging pilgrimage to the Holy Land' (*IDEA* magazine: July/August 2005), p10-11.

12. D. Johnson, Minister in charge St Philip's Leicester, *News and Views*, the Leicester Diocesan magazine, June 2005, p6.

13. *International Bulletin of Missionary Research*, January 2005. David B. Barrett and Todd M. Johnson give the statistically derived figure for the year 2004. It is not the sum of all verified cases. The definition of 'martyr' used is '. . . a believer in Christ who has lost his/her life prematurely, in a situation of witness, as a result of human hostility'.

14. The *Spectator*, article 'Church of Martyrs', 26 March 2005, p12 and Jamie Glazov, Symposium: The Muslim Persecution of Christians', *FrontPageMagazine.com*, 10 October 2003 http://frontpagemagazine.com/Articles/Printable.asp?ID=10242

15. Iqbal Sacranie in 'We must stand together as a nation' (*Daily Telegraph*: Friday 8 July 2005), p25.
16. *Grace Academy – losing to win* (Milton Keynes: Authentic, 2004), p105.
17. Christine A. Mallouhi, *Waging Peace on Islam* (Oxford: Monarch Books, 2000), p35-75, 314.

Chapter 4

Echoes of grace

Whatever is just and good in other religions finds its deepest meaning and its final perfection in Christ.
Pius XIII

As I learned to live in the rhythm of God's grace, I stopped trying to meet the imaginary expectations of God and my supporters in the UK. I found myself slipping into local culture more easily as the internal resistance to it lessened within me. I began to enjoy my salvation rather than endure it. In short, I was ready to stop being a Christian striver who was trying to help Muslim strivers to stop striving.

I moved from the theological seminary to teaching English as a foreign language, in classes where there was a good mix of Muslims and Orthodox Christians. In this environment my enquiry into grace was ready to move on to the Bible's influence on the Qur'an. In addition to lesson preparation, exam marking and Arabic lessons, I continued my investigation by looking for a reflection of biblical material in Islam. If I could find even an echo of grace in the Qur'an, it might be possible for enquiring

Muslims to use it; the Qur'an might point them to Jesus from within their Islamic context rather than having something imposed on them from outside.

A religion of Abraham

I found first that following in the footsteps of Abraham is deeply embedded in Muslim thinking. Muslims refer a lot to the 'Way of the Prophet' which is a concept rooted in Genesis.

> Abraham will surely become a great and powerful nation, and all nations on earth will be blessed through him. For I have chosen him, so that he will direct his children and his household after him to keep the *way of the LORD* by doing what is right and just, so that the LORD will bring about for Abraham what he has promised him. (Gen. 18:18-19)

Next I found that the early promise of God to Abraham provides Muslims with a sense of legacy they draw strength from. The Jew might understand the global aspect of being a 'blessing to the nations' in a spiritualized way but, for the Muslim, it becomes a mandate for Islamic mission in the world which parallels (for the Muslim) the Great Commission of Christ.

The next thing I discovered was that secular academics recognize historical and theological links between Judaism and Islam. Professor A. Geiger shows the importance of material about Abraham in the Rabbinic writings from which Muhammad derived the tradition that Abraham was the founder of the *ka'aba* at Mecca which became the focus of the *hajj* pilgrimage.[1] Peter Awm refers to a 'resonance' between the Qur'an and pre-Islamic non-canonical Jewish and Christian sources.[2]

Professor Sir Norman Anderson suggested anecdotally that the five times a day Islamic prayers correspond with the set times of Old Testament temple sacrifice. Jacques Jomier says that 'Islam always appeared as the Arab form of the eternal biblical religion i.e. Judaism.'[3] Colin Chapman sums the issue up.

> Muhammad must have absorbed something of the spirit and ritual of Jewish worship stories from the Old Testament and rabbinic legends. This should help us to understand not only the most obvious similarities between the doctrines of Judaism and Islam but also some of the deeper similarities between the spirit of the two religions.[4]

Bill Musk calls all three monotheistic faiths of Abraham – Judaism, Christianity and Islam – 'kissing cousins'.[5] Some claim that the similarities between Judaism and Islam were only true in the early days of Islam while others suggest the similarities are only cosmetic and that at a deeper level they prove to be significantly different. I was to find that this too had some truth to it.

When I asked Muslims what they believed, I found that they shared the same general overview (i.e. meta-narrative) about the world as Jews and Christians. For example, they believe in one Creator God (S25.2); Adam and Eve (S2.30-33); the devil and demons (S6.100,128; 72.1,15); the wilderness wanderings of Israel (S1.7; 2.40,97,102-103); heaven (S2.25; 3.15; 4.13); hell (S2.24; 3.10; 4.14); the second coming of Christ (S4. 159; 18.94, 98; 21.96); the resurrection of the dead (S2.28; 3.185); and the Virgin Mary, whom I found to be the most mentioned woman in the Qur'an (S2.87; 3.33; 4.156).

I saw that the Islamic understanding of God is akin to the more austere passages of the Old Testament. With this in mind, it made sense that the Qur'an claims to be a revelation *from* God rather than a revelation *of* God as in the Bible. In Islamic teaching God is unknowable. Muslim scholar Muhammad Hamidullah said, 'However close a man may approach God in his journeying towards him, even in his highest ascension, man remains man and very much remote from God.'[6] When Muslims actually read the Bible, they are faced with the grace story in which God *can be* known and is seen actively seeking relationship with humankind ever since the Garden of Eden where God called out for Adam (Gen. 3:8-9).

I was surprised to find that ten and a half out of the eleven Islamic tenets of faith and practice are biblical themes. I have included both the Qur'an and the Bible references below to demonstrate this.

Five pillars: *arkân al-islâm*

Muslims are required to observe five core actions which are referred to as religion (*dîn*). These pillars act like support columns to the edifice of Islam. As every Muslim observes them, Islam is upheld but if a Muslim fails to observe them, Islam is seen as being weakened or shamed – hence the reaction against dissidents.

1. Confession *shahâda* – i.e. of the God of Abraham (S2.116; 3.6,18,62; 4.87)
   Personal confession of that 'there is no god but God and Muhammad is His Messenger' – Christians disagree with the ending which includes Muhammad as the final Messenger (i.e. prophet) of God.
   – (1 Kgs. 8:33, 35; Mt. 10:32; Rom. 10:9; 14:11)

2. Prayer (*salât*)
   – (Gen. 20:17; Num. 11:2; 2 Chr. 7:14; Mt. 6:5,7; 1 Tim. 2:8; 1 Thes. 5:17)

3. Fasting (*sawm*) (S2.183-187)
   – (Ps. 35:13, 69:10; Jer. 36:6; Esth. 9:31; Neh. 9:1; Mt. 6:17)

4. Giving (*zakât*) (S2.271-273)
   – (Mt. 6:1–4; Acts 3:2)

5. Pilgrimage (*hajj*) (S2.196-197)
   – (Gen. 47:9; Ps. 119:54; Heb. 11:13)

There is a sixth item – *jihâd* or 'striving in the *way* of Islam'. Although this is not officially one of the pillars of Islam, in reality it is the foundation of all five pillars. This is because the five pillars are seen as an expression of the inward and spiritual, rather than the more familiar outward and military form of *jihâd*.

Six beliefs: imân al-islâm

Muslims are also required to believe six core things. These are their articles of faith (*imân*). When a Muslim holds these things in his belief, it is seen as mental submission to God. In Christian terms, this is loving the Lord with 'all your mind' (Mt. 22:37). The beliefs of Muslims are

1. God (*allah*) – the Unity of God (S37.35)
   – (Gen. 17:1, 35:11; Deut. 6:4; 1 Kgs. 8:33, 35; 2 Chr. 30:22; Mt. 10:32; Jn. 10:30; Rom. 10:9, 14:11)

2. The Angels (*mala'ikutuhu*) (S35.1)
   – (Gen. 22:11, 15; Deut. 6:4; Ps. 91:11, 104:4; Mt. 4:41)

3. The Holy Books (*kutubuhu*) (S2.177)
     i) Lost Scrolls of Abraham (*suhuf*) (S87.19)
    ii) Torah (*tawrât*) (S3.3, 48, 50, 65; 5.47; 23.49)
   iii) Psalms (*zabûr*) (S4.163; 17.55; 21.105)
    iv) Gospel (*injîl*) (S3.3, 48, 65; 5.46, 47,49)
     v) Qur'an (*qur'ân*) (S17.105)
   (Although Muslims do not normally own a Bible or
   have access to one, nevertheless they are taught to
   revere the three sections of the Bible listed above as
   subsidiaries to the Qur'an as the final revelation.)

4. The Prophets (*al-nabiim*) (S13.38; 14.4,9,15; 15.10; 35.24)
   Muslims believe there are 124,000 prophets which
   seems to reflect the 144,000 (Rev. 7).
   Around twenty-eight biblical characters are included
   in the Qur'an; including Job (S4.163); Noah (S2.33-34);
   Abraham (S2.124-27); Ishmael (S.127); Isaac (S2.123);
   Joseph (S6.84); Jacob (S2.132); Moses (S2.49,55,65; 3.11);
   Elijah (S6.85); David (S2.247); Solomon (S2.102);
   Jonah (S6.86) and Jesus (S2.87; 3.33; 4.156).

5. The Day of Judgement (*yawm uddîn*) (S2.62)
   – (1 Chr. 16:33; Is. 2:12; Joel 2:30-31; Mt. 10:15; Acts
   2:19-20; 2 Pet. 3:7, 10, 12; 1 Jn. 4:17)

6. The Decrees of God (*al-qâdir*) – i.e. the combination of
   all holy writ within the Islamic tradition
   – (Job. 22:28, 28:26; Ps. 2:7, 148:6; Prov. 4:26 [n.b. *shari'a*
   means right way]; Jer. 5:22; Mt. 4:4; Heb. 12:13)

By now I became concerned that this evidence was
leading me down a theologically liberal path. I was faced

with evidence which suggested that there is significant biblical content in Islamic teaching. I was also disturbed by the possibility that my simplistic perception was, in fact, wrong. John Stott said, 'An evangelical is not merely someone who believes all that the Bible teaches. An evangelical is someone who also believes whatever else the Bible may be found to teach.' This only partially reassured me because I now knew that some key Qur'anic ideas have their roots in the Bible but I was uncomfortable that the evidence required me to reassign Islam to a more positive mental category. If only Islam could be like Hinduism with more clear blue water between it and the Bible. At the intellectual level at least, I had little choice but to accept the fact that these links exist and must be accounted for. St Augustine of Hippo is reputed to have said, 'Truth, wherever it is to be found, it is the Lord's. Even the gold of Egypt is still gold.' If this is so, any truth locked up in Islam belongs to God and is therefore an open door for the Muslim. However, this did not help my internal conflict which was based on an emotional blockage. My attitude had to change before I could handle these facts objectively.

I came to the conclusion that Islam is more helpfully seen as an Arabized reflection of ancient Judaism. This accounted for the resonance I had always felt when talking to a Muslim. It was as though I was the eccentric anthropologist in the film *Jurassic Park* seeing his first real live dinosaur munching at the tops of trees and sensing the connection that spanned history. As I spoke with Muslims, I was struck by the fact that they are a living link with an Old Testament style religious community; a fact that helped my attitude towards them and provided a natural starting point in discussing the Gospel with them.

I found that various Orthodox Jewish practices are reflected in Islamic dogma. Both religions

- are spiritually rooted into the God of Abraham[7]
- are monotheistic – i.e. the Jewish *shama* 'One Lord' (Deut. 6:4) and the Muslim *kalima* 'No god but God'
- are governed by community law – *torah* and *shari'a*
- trace their law to a mountain – Mt Sinai and Mt Hirah (at Mecca)
- affirm the Ten Commandments (the Qur'an carries an equivalent for each one)
- are governed by a lunar calendar observing feasts according to the new moon
- observe dietary laws – *kosher* and *halal*
- are entered at conversion by a ritual bath, which is based on the Jewish *mikvah* (John the Baptist was from the Essene community which practised this form of immersion)
- have formed fundamentalist brotherhoods (see Acts 23:12-15)
- are partly in dispersion worldwide
- practise ritual ablutions (Ex. 40:30-32)
- practised a 'tribute' system with their captives (Deut 20:10-15; Josh. 16:10). This is paralleled by the Islamic *jizya* tax.
- are circumcised peoples according to the covenant of Abraham (Gen. 17)
- do not trim the edges of their beards (Lev. 21:5)
- are governed by holy text with related terminology e.g. Hebrew for 'chapter' is *shurah* while Arabic is *sura*.[8]

Sensitive and therefore (as yet) unpublished doctoral research suggests that

- the first chapter of the Qur'an (*al-fatiha*) may have originated from an Orthodox Christian hymn
- Lent may have been the precursor to the month-long fast of Ramadan for spiritual discipline

- the Islamic utterance known as the *bismil* declares *'bismillâh irrahmân irrahîm'* (in the Name of God the Merciful and the Compassionate). This is trinitarian and may be based on the Christian formulation 'in the Name of the Father, the Son and the Holy Spirit'. The word *'allah'* is the pre-Islamic Arabic for God; *'rahmân'* (merciful) an early Christian term used for Jesus and *'rahêm'* (compassionate) a term used for the Holy Spirit.

During a visit to a Coptic Orthodox monastery in the Sinai Peninsula, I discovered that the monks used the same positions of prayer as Muslims. They later explained to me that Muhammad first saw this pattern of biblical prostration in the monasteries when he travelled as a merchant. It was Muhammad who adopted the positions of Orthodox Christianity into Islam and not the other way round.

Christine Mallouhi recounts how she handed a Bible to Suha Arafat, the Christian Orthodox wife of the late Palestinian leader Yasir Arafat. Mrs Arafat stretched out both her hands to receive the Bible then instinctively kissed it to show her respect. This is a habit of Middle Eastern Christians and Muslims alike (my mind went back to the Moroccan circus worker who kissed the Gospel of Luke in Nottingham some years earlier).

On another occasion Christine was praying with western Christians who were working in a Muslim country. The eastern Christian traditions had so rubbed off on these westerners that after saying 'Amen' they went through the ritual of opening their hands, palms upward, in a posture of prayer before reverently wiping them over their faces. This symbolized the transmission of *baraka* (blessing). This was followed by a deferential touch of the chest over the heart.[9] To the uninitiated westerner these traditions may look like Islam influencing Christianity. However, on closer inspection, it becomes clear that it is the other way around.

Professor Norman Anderson said that 'The Qur'an resembles the Torah in the sense that it represents a strange combination of precept and prohibition, of religion and ethics.'[10] It seemed to me that if a Muslim were to read Leviticus and Numbers they would find parallels with Islamic law. This is because both *torah* and *shari'a* are systems of civil responsibility given *to* the people, *for* the people, to be enforced *by* the people. This was why Saul, a member of the religious establishment, guarded the coats of the members of the public while the common people carried out the Mosaic Law by stoning Stephen (Acts 7:58, 9:1).

It seemed to follow naturally that if this Judaistic DNA is embedded in Islam then the same issue of textualism and pharisaical legalism would also follow. I found that this is also the case.

> When people seek to live by guidelines given by God – in Torah or shari'a – one quick result seems to be an institutionalization of behaviour that focuses on the externals of law-keeping while ignoring the spirit of the law.[11]

I came to see that *shari'a* law and *torah* behave in a similar way. For example, the Torah treated all impurity, whether of spirit, soul or body, with as much caution as medical science treats germs today. The broad scope of the Mosaic Law is evident in Leviticus where instructions were given for spiritual, social, medical and moral aspects of life as follows:

Leviticus 11	health:	diet
12	medical:	childbirth and leprosy
13/14	hygiene:	leprosy and the sterilization of domestic items

15	sexuality	bodily discharges and the emission of semen
17	sanitary:	handling of animal blood
18	genetics:	rules of who can pro-create with whom
25	property:	fiscal and slavery laws

The rights that the Mosaic Law provided for the individual were balanced by the responsibilities it required from them. This reflects the covenantal nature of divine law; an arrangement is dependent upon the responses of two parties. It was not merely the dictate of God. This is why when the ancient Jews were in danger of deviating from the law, God coerced them to keep their part of the Covenant by exerting severe pressure on them (Deut. 8:19-20). Walking in God's ways in the law was the Old Testament way of 'keeping yourself in the love of God' (Jude 21). Violators were subject to seemingly excessive punishments which, to the western mind, are worthy of the Taliban. Take for instance the stoning to death of a man for breaking the Sabbath by collecting firewood (Num. 15:32-36) or the execution of a rebellious son who did not honour his father and mother (Deut. 21:18-21). We must bear in mind that God was dealing with his people in a different time and culture and that these draconian measures were fatherly discipline for the greater good of the holy community whose well-being was paramount (Deut. 8:5-9).

The focus of Islamic *shari'a* law is also on 'human conduct including food and drink, marriage, the family, morals, manners, trade and commerce, contracts, war and peace, *jihâd* and crime and punishment'.[12] This blurring of the distinction between the spiritual and physical world and the blending of law, theology and worship exists in the legal framework of both Jewish *torah* and Islamic *shari'a*. Kenneth Cragg comments . . .

Islam understands law as religion, religion as law ... Law, rather than theology, has the prior emphasis in Islam. Broadly, it is obedience to the will of God rather than fellowship in the knowledge of God's nature, which is paramount. Revelation is for direction of life, rather than disclosure of mystery ... submission, rather than communion.[13]

Watching Muslims trying to live out *shari'a* is like a flashback to Old Testament times and what it might have looked like to live among ancient Hebrews. Likewise, the original aim of *shari'a* is to keep the Muslim in the right path of God but there was no New Covenant to follow it. It did not come naturally to me to think of the Old Testament Law as a grace-provision until I read the Old Testament more carefully and recognized that the Law was often eulogized. For example the psalmist sang:

> The law of the LORD is perfect,
> > reviving the soul.
> > The statutes of the LORD are trustworthy,
> > making wise the simple.
> The precepts of the LORD are right,
> > giving joy to the heart.
> > The commands of the LORD are radiant,
> > giving light to the eyes.
> The fear of the LORD is pure,
> > enduring forever.
> > The ordinances of the LORD are sure
> > and altogether righteous.
> They are more precious than gold,
> > than much pure gold;
> > they are sweeter than honey,
> > than honey from the comb.
>
> (Ps. 19:7-10)

It became clear that the Semitic culture and theological thought-pattern of the Old Testament is locked into the DNA of Islam. I became convinced that I was standing on solid biblical ground when I said that Islam was 'an Arabized form of Judaism'. However, I soon hit up against the problem that if Islam shared so many common elements with Judaism, then it could be a counterfeit version of it. Had Satan devised it in order to inoculate the Arabian peninsular of Muhammad's time against the truth of the Gospel? Theories I had heard in the UK and adopted as my own came flooding back. 'If you have enough truth mixed in with error, the error is harder to detect and easier to believe.' 'Like a flu vaccination, if you hear a slightly twisted version of the truth and become familiar with that, when you hear the real thing you are immunized against it.' I went into another crisis of uncertainty about which mental category to put Islam in. Islam was either

1. a serious reflection of the truth
2. a counterfeit of the truth
3. a gross distortion of the truth.

I also found that there are too many significant differences between Judaism and Islam for 2. and 3. to be correct so I had to decide the extent to which 1. was true, regardless of how far some Muslims have been unfaithful to it – a problem Christians also struggle with. As I got going with this, the first area of disagreement turned out to be the status given to Ishmael and Isaac in Islam and the Judeo-Christian traditions.

Ishmael in the divine plan?

As a Christian I traced my spiritual lineage from Abraham through Isaac to Christ (Gal. 4:21-32). Muslims trace their spiritual (and even genetic) lineage through Ishmael back to Abraham. As I talked with Muslims about this they would complain that all Christians emphasize Isaac to the detriment of Ishmael and that some Christians even denigrate Ishmael. I had to admit I had heard Christians refer to Ishmael as the 'bogus heir' and the 'carnal counterfeit' of a woman who was 'only Abraham's concubine'. Muslims would insist that Christians should give due recognition to Ishmael as Abraham's first-born son; a fact that carries special status in the cultures of the non-western world but especially in the Middle East.

This fact provoked me to find out what the Bible actually says about Ishmael's status, compared to Isaac's. I began in Genesis chapter sixteen where I found that not only was Sarah childless (Gen. 16:1) but infertile (Gen. 11:30). She needed not just IVF but a miracle, because childlessness was (and still is) a social catastrophe in eastern cultures. A follower of Jesus from a Muslim background told me how she was summarily divorced for having a string of miscarriages and stillbirths.

So would the solution to Sarah's crisis be by self-help (i.e. works) or by divine assistance (i.e. grace)? Sarah and Abraham chose the self-help route (Gen. 16:2) and made Hagar, Sarah's Egyptian maid, a second wife to Abraham (Gen. 16:3b). Although she was a second wife, she was also the mother of Abraham's first-born son Ishmael (Gen. 16:4a). I noted how the self-help solution (Gen. 16:2b) introduced 'works' into the DNA of the household and from then on the works/grace tension can be observed through the rest of the Bible.

Hagar's pregnancy triggered rivalry with Sarah (Gen. 16:4) until Hagar was forced out of the household to live in the desert. This is a powerful symbol of the need for us to extend an invitation to the sons of Ishmael (i.e. the Arabs) and all non-Arab Muslims to leave their self-effort and return to the household of faith (Gen. 25:12-18).

> The call of the minaret must always be, for the Christian, a call to retrieval. The objective is not, as the Crusaders believed, the repossession of what Christendom once lost, but the restoration to Muslims of the Christ whom they have always missed.[14]

The 'angel of the LORD' approached Hagar in the desert (Gen. 16:7). This indicated God's sovereign intention that Ishmael should survive. The 'angel of the Lord' (*malakh ha elohîm*) literally means the 'angel *which is* the LORD'. Some scholars understand this to be a 'Christophany' or a pre-incarnate appearance of the Lord Jesus Christ.[15] Assuming this was true, it made this high-level encounter of Hagar's a doubly significant milestone in God's plans in human history.

The angel told Hagar to return to the household and 'submit' there (Gen. 16:9), which she did. It is a curious coincidence that the angel should use a word that translates into English as 'submit'. This is the Arabic word *tislem* – the imperative or command form of the word *islam* (submission) and from which the word *muslim* is derived, to identify someone who is a submitter to God. This is a perfectly biblical concept.[16] In effect, the angel was instructing Hagar to return and do her *islam* within the household of Abraham. She does so and Ishmael was born. He was circumcised at the age of thirteen, along with Abraham and the other males of the household (Gen. 17:23).

When Isaac was born, the friction started up again; this time between the mothers and their sons (Gen. 21:9). Now, Hagar was driven out of the household for good, with Sarah's words ringing in her ears 'Get rid of the bond woman and her son' (Gen. 21:10). These words were also used by some of the Crusader knights in their unsuccessful bid to retake Jerusalem from Turkish Muslims in the Middle Ages.

The more I discussed Ishmael with Muslims, the more I realized that I had to decide how, as a Christian, I ought to rank him in the scheme of things. I found that the stress Muslims put on Ishmael's rights was indeed justified biblically. If I were still under any illusions about it, the matter was made doubly clear by the fact that God saved Ishmael's life not once but twice (Gen. 16:7-14; 21:19); God also remained with Ishmael in his bedouin lifestyle (Gen. 21:20a). I realized that if God had wanted to stop the emergence of Muhammad and therefore Islam he only needed to end Ishmael's line there and then – but he did not. God went on to be totally faithful to Ishmael and made a nation from him – simply because he was Abraham's son (Gen. 21:13). Ishmael also became the father of twelve sons (Gen. 17:20) which was paralleled later by Jacob's twelve sons (Gen. 35:23-26).

In Genesis 17 Abraham pleaded with God to overlook his self-effort and accept Ishmael as the means of fulfilling the covenantal promise (Gen. 17:18). It is possible that Abraham may have genuinely thought that God intended to fulfil his original promise through Ishmael. However, in the end God left Abraham in no doubt by insisting that the 'everlasting covenant' (i.e. the gospel of grace) would belong to Isaac's line (Gen. 17:21) from which Christ was born and which brought the promised blessing to 'all nations' (Gen. 12:3). It is significant that, of all the offspring, it was Isaac and Ishmael who laid their father Abraham to rest (Gen. 25:9). Ishmael was second only to Isaac in a hierarchy of Abraham's male offspring[18]

1. Sarah and Isaac – Recipient line of the 'everlasting covenant' and inherited *all* from Abraham (Gen. 17:19, 21,25:5)
2. Hagar and Ishmael – recipient line of personalized blessing (Gen. 17:20)
3. Keturah (Zimran, Jokshan, Medan, Midian, Ishbak and Shuah) – (Gen. 25:1-2)
4. Concubines (unnamed sons) – sent away from Isaac (Gen. 25:6)

Isaac's descendants included the Jewish Old Testament prophets who produced the Scriptures that were also to become officially recognized in Islam, as we have seen earlier in the list of holy books. By contrast, Ishmael's line produced no prophets or Scripture until Muhammad was born at Mecca in AD 570. The Islamic statement of faith says, 'There is no god but God and Muhammad is His Messenger.' This reference to an Arabian messenger could be read as a subtle hint at the correction of the imbalance or even the regaining of respect after a period of shame for the sons of Ishmael. The sub-text suggests that God's latest and final Messenger 'is one of us'. This need to restore Arab honour began the steady drift of the Muslim community away from its monotheistic cousins, Judaism and Christianity.

The worldwide Muslim community (*umma*) has continued its quest for an identity that is distinct from Jews and Christians. The official direction of Islamic prayer (*qibla*) was changed from Jerusalem, where it began, to Mecca. Islamic traditions have sprung up around some of the biblical and qur'anic incidents such as the Muslim claim that Abraham was going to sacrifice Ishmael, not Isaac, even

though the Qur'an does not actually say it was Ishmael
(S37.83-113).

Another tradition developed which says that the Bible was
changed. 'A party of them (Jews) heard the Word of God and
perverted it knowingly after they understood it' (S2.75). Even
if taken at face value, the verse does not appear to support the
enormous weight put on it by many Muslims. I could see that
the verse probably referred to the casual practice of Jewish
Scripture rather than the Scripture itself.

In more recent centuries there has been increasing
defensiveness by both Muslims and Christians about the
similarities and differences between the two faiths. It
became apparent to me that the bad attitude that had
developed between Christians and Muslims had become
the real problem. It is not the content of the argument
between Christians and Muslims that is the issue but the
attitude which lies behind the arguments.

> Islam developed in an environment of imperfect Christianity
> and later by its own force it became and remained at odds
> with the pure faith of Christ beyond the Church's imperfec-
> tion. This is the tragedy of the rise of Islam, which claims to
> displace what it has never really known.[18]

The original ethnic Arabs of the Arabian Gulf are technically
neither Jew nor Gentile. They constitute a third category
because they are not sons of Isaac yet, unlike Gentiles, many
of their tribes are genetic descendants of Abraham. Some
researchers refer to this peculiar state of affairs as the
'Ishmaelitish mystery'; something Christians must deal with.

Clearly if Islam's arrival in the world was approved by
God then Islam can only be properly understood by those
who are able to interpret it through a theological view of
history rather than a secularist philosophical view of
history. I came to believe that the solution to the question

of Islam (if there is one) will be found firstly by Christians rather than politicians. It is only when history is understood biblically that we recognize how inextricably linked it all is to Jesus Christ who reconciled back the inhabitants and the affairs of the world to himself on the Cross and will ultimately subdue everything under himself (Col. 1:15-17, 20).

Islam's core differences

Next I looked in detail at other core issues where Islam disagrees with Christianity. I found it more helpful to ask myself what Muhammad's original intention was in each point of contradiction and how it was intended to guide the Muslim. I identified the list of objections below to be the most pertinent in highlighting Islam's contradiction of biblical teaching.

1. The Oneness of God

The Bible reveals God in three persons, which have become known as the Trinity. I had been told that Islam denies the existence of the Trinity. I noticed that in Sura 4.171-2 the Qur'an claims that Christians believe in three Gods and that this is wrong. I am a Christian and I knew that the Bible teaches the existence of one God revealed in three persons – Father, Son and Holy Spirit. So technically speaking Islam was not denying the Trinity but the notion of 'tri-theism' or 'polytheism'. I concluded that the real issue here is the mutual misunderstanding about what is supposed to be believed by Christians and what is supposed to be denied by Muslims. It seemed to me that Muslims baulk at the Trinity while many Christians dutifully struggle to understand it.

2. *Jesus Christ as the Son of God*

I had been told that Islam denies that Jesus is the Son of God yet I found that the Qur'an teaches the virgin birth (S21.91). I then read in Sura 6.95-101 that God could not have a physical union and beget a son nor would he adopt one (see also S19.88-98). The original intention here was positive in that it was safeguarding the integrity of Mary as a virgin and of Jesus as Messiah, in the face of the rejection of both by the Arabian Jews of Muhammad's day. It was a surprise to Muslims when I told them that Christians actually agree with this safeguard and that the Bible does not teach a sexual union between God and Mary. This opened up the way for me to explain that 'Son of God' is a spiritual title, not a physical description. I used to describe Jesus as 'the Word of God in flesh' with no problem. Again the problem seems to be one of mis-communication over what is supposed to be believed by Christians and what is supposed to be denied by Muslims.

3. *Jesus' death on the Cross*

The Qur'an states that Jesus did not die on the Cross (S4.157). It goes on to explain that 'they were under the illusion that they had crucified him'. This is an attempt to refute the claim that Jesus was defeated. I noted too that there is also an allusion to Jesus' resurrection (S4.158). Underlying the denial of crucifixion is the Islamic theme of power and the belief that no prophet of God could be humiliated in this way, hence the attempt to resist claims that Jesus was tortured and executed. This desire to defend Jesus' reputation can also be seen as believing the wrong thing for the right reason.

4. The purpose of the Qur'an

Muslims claim the Qur'an to be the final and superlative revelation from God, which makes the Bible redundant. The Qur'an looks to the Bible for its validation (S2.53:3.93-94; 10.94-95; 29.46). However, if Islam carries a reflection of Judaism and therefore echoes of the Old Testament, the Qur'an may become a stepping-stone to the Bible. Scholar Giulio Basetti-Sani was a help to me in this respect when he argued that, 'It is proper that the Church interpret the Qur'an. Just as she has the "key" to interpret the Old Testament, she also has the "key" for the correct explanation of the Qur'an'.[19] The Qur'an is helpfully understood in part at least as a commentary on Jewish Scripture and a correction to inadequate Judaism which Muhammad saw as being flouted by the Arabian Jews of his time.

5. Muhammad as the final and greatest prophet

I thought Muhammad was a sinister character but when I began to set him in his social context, it helped me see why his form of religion and morality was steeped in the mindset of *torah*. Muhammad's leadership genius sadly turned to brutality later on which was in keeping with the Old Testament culture in the Arabia of his day.

Muhammad's primary audience included these Arabized Jews, whose unorthodox practice of Judaism he challenged. His mission appeared to be an attempt to bring such Jews back to authentic Judaism. The Arabs could then be summoned out of idolatry and into this purer form of faith. In short, Muhammad's mission was originally a kind of apostleship to the Jews and so the Arabizing of Judaism in the Arabian Peninsula and the calling of Arabs into the pure faith of Abraham.[20]

When the Jews and Christians rejected Muhammad's prophethood and message, he reacted with hurt and anger. Originally Muhammad was neither anti-Jewish nor anti-Christian *per se* but he did reject 'heterodox' or unorthodox practices. Eventually he turned against the Jews and Christians because they rejected him. In doing so, he overreacted to the most vital tenets of Christianity as listed above; possibly because he did not understand them. What I could conclude about Muhammad, however, was that although I did not accept him as comparable to Jesus, nevertheless I did recognize that he was instrumental in bringing the pagan and idolatrous tribes of Arabia from being 'afar off' from the purposes and covenants of God to being 'nearer' (Acts 2:39); a feat I came to thank God for because it made it easier to convey the Gospel to a 'Judaized' person than a secular materialist.

6. Islam and the sovereignty of God

Up to this point I had been unable to fit the rise of Islam into my mental framework. As a result I relegated it to the area of dark eschatology and Daniel's dream of the powers that would dominate the earth (Dan. 2). I was comfortable with consigning Muslims to the realm of conspiracy theories and thought Muhammad was a candidate for the False Prophet of the book of Revelation. Then I found myself rapidly unlearning this sort of thing. I discovered that Islam is difficult to place in end-time biblical prophecy but came to realize that this could be because it may not be an issue by the time the end comes. Nor could I find anything in the Bible that supports the view that Muhammad could be identified with the False Prophet. In fact, I found the opposite – the False Prophet did 'lying signs and wonders' and led people *away* from

God (Rev. 19:20) while Muhammad never performed a miracle and tried to bring people *to* the God of Abraham.

I began to see Islam, not as a counterfeit of biblical truth but as an inadequate parallel manifestation of it. If we do use the word 'distortion' about Islam, it can only be a distortion of New Testament revelation rather than Old Testament. In this sense, Islam is not a distortion but an attempt at faithfulness to the limited Old Testament light it has received. My conclusion was that Islam differs from its early Jewish roots in degree rather than kind.

Although Ishmael was subject to certain blessings in the economy of God, he will always remain a child of 'human effort' (Gal. 4.23). To my mind, Islam is less about demonic doctrines masquerading as truth and more about being a non-western politico-religious movement. I have gone on record elsewhere as saying that Islam will always be more 'humanly conceived than divinely inspired'.[21]

As a Christian participant in an Islamic society, I began to appreciate that Islam (like everything else) is surrounded by the sovereignty of God. I had to admit, too, that my view of time was western and therefore linear rather than eastern and cyclical. The cyclical view of history is the stuff of biblical prophecy and its repeated fulfilments. This was why, to many Muslims, the Crusades seem like last year. To the westerner the fact that Muhammad was born *after* Jesus chronologically throws our way of thinking into confusion. How could God allow such a challenger to the claims of Christ to emerge after the birth of the church?

I satisfied myself with the knowledge that we shall know the answer to this by and by but I also found that although Muhammad was born post-New Testament he was Old Testament in his message. As a result Caldicott sees Islam as akin to the continuing significance of the Jews. Islam is prolonging the Old Covenant dispensation of the ancient people of Israel. The prayer challenge to Christians is that the house of Ishmael (the Muslims), like the house of Isaac (the Jews), still exists outside the 'Everlasting Covenant' of salvation by grace.

Why was Judaism never absorbed into Christianity. Was this also divine providence? Just as the dispensation of Israel continued after the birth of the church, so Islam belongs to the same dispensation as Judaism. It awaits its completion in Christ.

Islam (can be seen) as a message akin in some ways to that of John the Baptist, who was sent "in the spirit of Elijah" to prepare the way for the arrival of the Son of Man on the clouds of glory at the end of time.[22]

'Even though Islam is chronologically AD and has had fourteen centuries of contact with Christianity, it remains informationally BC.[23] For political and human reasons, Islam's Old Testament understanding has never managed to move forward to find its logical completion in Christ. The role of a Christian who discusses the Good News with a Muslim is therefore similar to Priscilla and Aquila assisting Apollos to understand the faith more adequately (Acts 18:24-26). The Muslim has received only the reflected light of the Qur'an which acts like the moon. I believe this light is gained from the Bible, which acts like the sun.

The outcome of my research brought me finally to the same position as Basetti-Sani who saw Islam as a 'less than ideal path that leads in the general direction of Christ'. However, he qualified this by clarifying that Islam is 'not an economy of salvation parallel (or indeed equal) to that of Christ'.

Logic tells us that all roads do not lead to God and I certainly found no evidence to suggest that salvation is on offer in Islam as it is in the Gospel. However, what I did find was that a Muslim, like the Orthodox Jew, may be part of the way down the right road towards Christ, without realizing it themselves. Islam has the potential to pre-evangelize the Muslim. I use the expression 'pre-evangelize' to convey the sensitization to the issues of the Gospel which Muslims subconsciously receive through Islamic dogma on the weakness of human nature and our inability to please God without help. This predisposes them, under the Holy Spirit's influence, to enquire further when they hear the Gospel or see it fleshed out by someone who models the life of Christ.

A Muslim friend said to me, 'Brother Steve, you're a better Muslim than I have ever been.' He could see something in me that he felt he was supposed to have but did not. I believe he was picking up an echo of grace as it resonated through my life. It was as though his soul had heard a song once, then forgotten it but was now being reminded of it. He did not know it but he was agreeing with the Apostle Paul who pointed out that, by grace, Gentiles who live without any religious law 'by nature do the things required by the law. They show that the requirements of the law are written on their hearts' (Rom. 2:14-15).

Basetti-Sani urged Christians to help Muslims retrace their steps to wherever their 'march to Christ' got diverted. This way of engaging with the Qur'an has the potential to release any embedded echoes of grace in it and to help the Muslim.

St Paul speaks of the 'veil', which falls between the reader and the Old Testament, with the result that Jesus was not believed in (cf. 2 Cor. 3:14-16). An analogous veil prevents the Muslim from seeing the true and authentic Christ.

Can the Muslim discover in the Qur'an the real meaning of its message as being oriented towards the 'good news' of the gospel? The Muslim will realize that he is being given true enrichment because he is not asked to look elsewhere, except in the book that he accepts as his only criterion of truth.[25]

The issue for me was not whether or not the parallels between Islam and Judaism actually exist but what the implications were of the fact that they did. For example:

- Islam is an Abramic faith, which means that it differs from Judaism only in degree but not in kind. The two faiths share similar DNA as they are of the same kind. This also makes Islam a second cousin to Christianity.
- Rather than calling Islam a 'counterfeit of Judaism' it is closer to a 'variation on the theme' of Judaism. As such, Judaism should be seen by Christians as a vital meeting point in any discussion between a Christian and a Muslim.
- On the basis of the above, to relegate Islam to the same category as other world religions is not an option. Islam cannot be conveniently put on the back-burner as something 'other' to be thought about at some time – if ever.
- Islam exists and Christians need to come to terms with that and to tease out the similarities and differences between Islam and Christianity and then form a biblically informed opinion about the facts rather than the negative bias so often expressed in popular Christian pulp-fiction.
- Christians need to co-operate with the Spirit of God by relating to Muslims from a position of confident humility and grace, in order to communicate the Good News to them.

The net result of my investigation was that I became more confident in relating to Muslims. I was able to understand and handle both their positive and negative reactions because a sufficiently strong relational bridge had been built between me and them. This meant that some heavy-duty spiritual hardware could be wheeled across for my Muslim friend to inspect.

Mini-breakthroughs started to happen in my daily routine. My approach had not changed but my attitude had. Fawziyya, a young Muslim woman who was fashionable and secular, taught English in my department. She suddenly needed understanding and support after she was scarred for life in a road accident on a Sinai desert road. Fawziyya started wearing the *hijab* head scarf as a sign of her thankfulness to God for sparing her life and also as an expression of repentance and her desire to return to Islam for protection. As far back as the Gospel accounts, Middle Easterners have equated misfortune with divine punishment. When Jesus encountered a blind person it prompted others to ask, 'Who has sinned, this man or his parents?' (Jn. 9:1-3). Fawziyya needed Jesus to walk with her during her difficult experience and she found solace in the person of one of his followers. In doing this, Fawziyya took a step closer to Christ.

Then there was Khaled, a Kuwaiti student from a wealthy family. He was having a minor operation and Arab males can get squeamish about these things. Khaled was terrified. The night before he was due to be admitted to a private hospital, he stayed behind after class to confide in me about his fear. I loaned him an Arabic New Testament (*injîl*) and pointed him to Jesus' words, 'I am the resurrection and the life. Anyone who believes in me will live, even though they die. And whoever lives by believing in me shall never die' (Jn. 11:25-26). Needless to say, Khaled survived the operation and in the process he also took a step closer to Christ.

On another occasion a Muslim friend who had been secretly reading a Bible told me, 'Your book is not like our book. Your book is the only book I've ever read that reads me.' He started reading because I urged him that as a Muslim, the Bible was his book too and that he needed to see what the Qur'an was referring to. His incredible statement was a testimony to the power of the Bible, which resonated for him in a way that he had not experienced before.

All this was firing me up with passion and faith for ordinary Muslims at their point of felt need. It had taken God a decade to give me a change of mind and heart towards Muslims. I did not realize it at the time but I was now just about to receive a huge set-back that would change not just me, but the whole course of my life.

Notes

1. Abraham Geiger, *Judaism and Islam*, English translation F. M. Young (Madras: MDC SPCK, 1898), p96.
2. Peter Awm, *Satan's Tragedy and Redemption – Iblîs in Sufi Psychology* (Leiden: E. J. Brill, 1983), p20-21.
3. Jacques Jomier, *How to Understand Islam* (Crossroad Publishing, 1990).
4. Colin Chapman, *Cross and Crescent – Responding to the challenge of Islam* (Leicester: IVP, 1995), p266.
5. Bill A. Musk, *Kissing Cousins? – Christians and Muslims face to face* (Oxford: Monarch Books, 2005).
6. Muhammad Hamidullah, Introduction to Islam (Paris: Centre Culturel Islamique, 1969) in Colin Chapman, *Cross and Crescent* (Leicester: IVP, 1995), p226.
7. Tony Payne, *Islam in our Backyard – a novel argument* (Mathias Media, 2002). 'Much of what Islam teaches about

Allah is recognisable to Jews and Christians – and indeed to secular westerners whose culture has been shaped by Judeo-Christian foundations.' For a fuller treatment of the issue of Allah as God of the Bible see *Friendship First – the Manual* (Market Rasen: Friendship First Publications, 2003), Appendix 6, p82-83.

8. Montgomery Watt, *Bell's Introduction to the Qur'an* (Edinburgh: 1970), p57-58.

9. Christine A. Mallouhi, *Waging Peace on Islam* (Oxford: Monarch Books, 2000), p312-313.

10. Norman Anderson, *God's Law and God's Love – an essay on Comparative religion* (London: Collins, 1980), p75.

11. Bill A. Musk, *Kissing Cousins? – Christians and Muslims face to face* (Oxford: Monarch Books, 2005), p360.

12. Badru D. Kateregga and D. Shenk, *A Muslim and a Christian in Dialogue* (Scotsdale: Herald Press, 1997), p81.

13. Kenneth Cragg, *Islam and the Muslim* (Open University Press, 1978), p49.

14. Kenneth Cragg, *op cit*, p245-246.

15. Harris, Archer and Waltke et al, *Theological Wordbook of the Old Testament* (Chicago: Moody Press, 1980), p464.
The angel of the Lord' is understood to be God because he speaks for God in the first person (Gen. 16:10; Ex. 3:2; Judg. 2:1) and he took the intercessory role with God on behalf of humankind (Zech. 1:12; 3:1-5).

16. Submission to God, and one another, is a New Testament theme; see for example – Hebrews 13:17; James 4:7; 1 Peter 2:13,18;3:1;5:6.

17. Bill A. Musk *Kissing Cousins? – Christians and Muslims face to face* (Oxford: Monarch Books, 2005), p42.

18. Kenneth Cragg, *The Call of the Minaret* (London: Collins Flame Classics, 1986), pp245-246.

19. Giulio Basetti-Sani, *The Koran in the Light of Christ – a Christian Interpretation of the Sacred Book of Islam* (Chicago: Franciscan Herald Press, 1977), p101,102.

20. Giulio Basetti-Sani, *The Koran in the Light of Christ – a Christian Interpretation of the Sacred Book of Islam* (Chicago: Franciscan Herald Press, 1977), p30.

21. Steve Bell, *Friendship First – the Manual* (Market Rasen: Friendship First Publications, 2003), p8.
22. Stratford Caldicott, 'His Seed Like Stars: The Dialogue Between Christians and Muslims' (*Second Spring* magazine, 2002), p31-34.
23. Charles Kraft, *Christianity in Cross-cultural Perspective – A Study in Dynamic Biblical Theologising* (Maryknoll NY: Orbis, 1981), p402.
24. Giulio Basetti-Sani, *The Koran in the Light of Christ – a Christian Interpretation of the Sacred Book of Islam* (Chicago: Franciscan Herald Press, 1977), p35.
25. Giulio Basetti-Sâni, *The Koran in the Light of Christ – a Christian Interpretation of the Sacred Book of Islam* (Chicago: Franciscan Herald Press, 1977), p105.

Chapter 5

Grace in East and West

'Amor dat novos oculos' Love gives new eyes
St Augustine

Something was not quite right. I had just arrived back
home in Cairo after a trip via Kuwait to northern India. It
was 1990 and almost the tenth anniversary of my arrival
in Egypt. I sensed something was wrong but I could not
put my finger on it. Then strange things started to
happen.

Whenever I picked up the phone in my apartment, I
could hear someone breathing at the other end. The
phone was being tapped. My mail started arriving more
slowly: some would be opened and re-sealed and some
pieces disappeared. On several occasions, as I would
come and go from my apartment building, I passed a
man wearing a dark crumpled suit and a tie, hanging
around in the entrance.

Then one day a piece of paper appeared in my pigeon-
hole just inside the entrance to the apartment block. It
was typed and in English. I went cold as I read the
summons to appear for 'interview' at the office of the

mubâhez (Intelligence Service). This is effectively the Secret Police, whose headquarters at the time were in an attractive downtown suburb which hugged the east bank of the River Nile. The date and time of the interview were specific, with no alternatives offered. Failure to turn up was not an option.

The appointment was at 10:30pm and I had alerted people to pray. I arrived in the semi-deserted building and sat for what felt like an eternity, rehearsing in my mind what they might ask and how I would answer. When the time came for me to go in, I was both surprised and unnerved at the relaxed and friendly atmosphere. I was offered a cup of tea would have been lulled into a false sense of security had I not been warned that these men were trained by the American government in the art of western-style information extraction. There were three of them. One did most of the talking, the second dropped in some questions, while the third said nothing and just sat there scrutinizing me ominously.

They assured me that they were just checking facts and wanted to put a human face to the picture and information they had in their file on me. This was something I did not even know existed until that moment. The whole thing was over in just under three quarters of an hour. I left feeling the sense of relief you might feel after a driving test – regardless of whether you had passed or failed.

My routine returned to normal until a few weeks later when I was called in again. This appointment was at 11:00pm and the procedure much the same as before, except that it took an hour. During this time they divulged more of what they knew about me and what they called my 'Christian activities'. A discussion followed in which I felt irritated by their attitude to me being an active Christian. They inferred that I was a Christian version of an Islamic fundamentalist and therefore in need of their scrutiny. I managed to survive the second 'tea party' but in the expatriate community they had a saying, 'One visit to the police is routine, two is ominous but three means it's time to pack your bags.'

I was apprehensive in case a third summons came. One month later it did. I returned to my apartment after work to find another summons in my pigeon-hole. 'This is it,' I thought to myself. A knot developed in my stomach. I duly attended the appointment at 10:30pm and was interviewed more formally; this time by two of the three previous men. However, there was a new and more senior third man. I was referred to as a 'missionary', to which I said I was just being a Christian and that a Muslim ought to appreciate that. This point was going nowhere and I knew it.

The session was tense and it felt longer than the others. In reality it lasted just twenty minutes. I walked out into the night air and looked for a taxi home knowing that I had not heard the last from these people. I was summoned to see my section head at work. This large and imposing man with pharaonic features was annoyed with me for causing him problems and he curtly informed me that there would be no work permit for me in the following term or ever again. The police did not even have the courtesy to inform me themselves. I had three months to leave the country before being escorted to the airport when my current work permit expired.

I went through a storm of emotional and mental battles. It was so unjust to expel someone who had developed a healthy respect for Muslims. Having taken great strides in my attitude to Islam, I was now at the receiving end of an Islamic police state. I became angry, then hurt and then sad.

I used my last three months to pack up my apartment and tie up loose ends. I took my time saying goodbyes to people and to Cairo. I visited sites I had never had time to go to and made a mini-pilgrimage to favourite spots that offered panoramic views over the sprawling city. Having freighted my belongings, the time eventually came for me to get on a plane myself. By now I was depressed. What was I going to do? How could this messy departure be a part of God's plan for me and where was he leading me now?

On arrival at Heathrow in the Spring of 1991, I made my way to Nottingham where I lodged with friends. During my first few months back in Britain I felt I had become an onlooker in my own culture. I felt very Middle Eastern and apparently I sounded like it, too, because people who knew me well commented on the fact that I was speaking English with a touch of the Arabic staccato pattern. This was the effect of pronouncing Arabic as well as speaking Arabized English to my students. I was pining for the more familiar ways of the Middle East. My bodily reflexes were Middle Eastern: I kept saluting people as a gesture of respect.

Later on I recognized this re-entry experience as something called 'reverse culture-shock'. Would the same grace that kept me in the East keep me in the West? The answer was 'yes' because eventually I did find 'grace to help in time of need' (Heb. 4:16); though it took me two years to readjust.

During my first year back in Britain I thought about my next step and considered teaching English in a Gulf State and an invitation to teach English in north west China where there are twenty-two million Muslims. Neither of these proved right but then I met someone at a prayer conference for the Muslim world and plans quickly developed for me to become Director of Carey

Grace for Muslims?

College, a non-residential unit that offered group interactive training for ordinary Christians. This facility was set up by a partnership of mission groups. The aim was to provide study material for home-groups on Islam and Christian witness. This was an opportunity for me to begin the process of systematizing the issues in a way that enabled western Christians to connect with them.

The East/West divide

As my readjustment to British life continued, I found that significant changes had been taking place during my absence. People no longer spoke about 'Muslims in Britain' but 'British Muslims' which indicated a shift in thinking. As the children and grandchildren of the first Muslim immigrants became a significant subsection of the population they became recognized as indigenous Britons; the immigration issue was now more about asylum seekers and refugees.

I noticed too that the press had devised the collective title 'the Muslims', irrespective of nationalities. I wondered what this generic title was suggesting. I never heard the Indian community referred to as 'the Hindus' so clearly the public perception of the Muslim had changed. What used to be seen as exotic now tended to be seen as potentially sinister. Those once regarded as a lot of individuals were now seen as a group to be reckoned with and this was making white people feel slightly uncomfortable.

An East/West clash of ideologies was developing as western leaders, whether intentionally or not, gave the impression that the rest of the non-western world was in some sense a less 'civilized' extension of the West. The best of the West was compared with the worst of 'the rest', which made me defensive about the non-western way. I also came across westerners who took for granted the Judeo-Christian influence that contributed to the West while dismissing as irrelevant the biblical principles that have under-girded its so-called 'progress' for centuries. Muslims, on the other hand, would argue that western decadence was a by-product of the same Judeo-Christian heritage that westerners were taking for granted. All this made me feel like a 'go-between' because in reality I could see good and bad on both sides.

One reason for the East/West miscommunication is that no Muslim country has undergone an Enlightenment period as Europe did. I knew that the assumptions of the West are linked to that period; for example the freedom of speech, assembly, religious affiliation, individual choice and political opinion, the notion of civil rights and the predisposition towards humanitarianism. It was clear to me that the traditional values of eastern cultures are culturally closer to the European Middle Ages. These societies still have complex class systems, strictly defined gender roles, an emphasis on modesty, strict sexual norms, a low status for animals, a more rigid enforcement of punishment for crime, the prescribed observance of religion, authoritarian forms of government and the restriction of the freedom of expression. This East/West divide was very obvious to me when I heard British people judge eastern values, calling them 'draconian', while British Muslims I spoke to were proud of their traditional values because they are closer to the divine requirements prescribed in the Qur'an.

My life and travels outside Europe helped me appreciate the positives of the Enlightenment, the Reformation and the Industrial Revolution, all of which shaped life in the West. However, they also made me cautious about the corresponding negative effect of western sophistication and self-reliance. Such negatives included the western perception that we have 'come of age' and therefore no longer need God. There was also a new morality of convenience that was coming into vogue in the Eurozone. This required tolerance of everything except the Judeo-Christian heritage as traditional Christian values came under threat from aggressive secularism which was becoming the preferred moral and spiritual foundation for European societies, replacing its Judeo-Christian past.

The late Great Britain

I found myself identifying more with the values of British Muslims than I did with indigenous white Britons. The nation was not in particularly good shape and it was the Muslims who seemed to realize it more than secular Britons. This indicated to me that Muslims may be more of an ally than a foe, particularly in the area of biblical moral values.

After the litany of problems I have outlined in the East it was now the West's turn to get a bad mark. The moral basis in the Muslim communities of Britain won my respect. My absence from the country had sensitized me to the fact that following the so-called 'swinging sixties' Britain had changed, as a result of a number of factors including the increased breakdown of the family, greater affluence, more social mobility, growing secularism and the continued decline of Christianity in national life. Britain had become only culturally Christian; a process that had been going on for fifty years as successive governments had legalized the breaking and/or the rationalizing of most of the Ten Commandments.[1] I was not happy about the condition of the Britain I had returned to and I felt allied to the Muslims I met and spoke with about this.

Significant numbers of Muslims arrived in Britain over several decades assuming that the moral values held by all Britons corresponded with their idea of 'Christian'. Unfortunately they found Britain to be an increasingly secular society. As a Christian, I could understand why most Muslims I talked to resisted becoming integrated into the ungodly aspects of British life. Having returned from life in a Muslim society, I could empathize with British Muslims who had come from nations where faith was dominant and religion was a more robustly practised part of life. This is one of the issues that gives western Muslims their sense of superiority over the so-called 'Christians' they think they are living among.

It did not come as a total surprise to me to find that British Muslims were coming to the conclusion that Christianity is a failed religion, responsible for allowing Britain to become decadent. I disagreed with their conclusion but could see how they had reached it. These Muslims genuinely thought that Islam could do a better job of running a Britain that was beginning to struggle with 'yob-culture', anti-social behaviour and binge drinking. As I write, a news item is breaking about a three-year-old girl who was abducted by three men, one of whom (a twenty-six-year-old) was later charged with raping her. At times like this I feel ashamed to be British and can understand why Muslims react to this and other sorts of crime less common in Muslim nations, although corruption and physical abuse may be more common in the Muslim world.

Exposure to African Islam

By late 1992 I had been head-hunted from Director of Carey College to the post of International Director of Action Partners Ministries (formerly Sudan United Mission). For the next nine years, my life was deeply influenced by the role of Islam among the peoples of the African Sahel. I observed first hand how the life and practice of these Muslims were heavily underpinned by animistic rituals from the African traditional religions which are overlayed by Islam. I observed, too, how Islam and Christianity negotiated for space to co-exist. I was pleased to be working with Action Partners because the sub-Saharan belt that runs from Somaliland to Senegal is a crucial part of the world 'where the Church and Islam meet'.[2]

It was a challenging area of the world to practice a grace response to Muslims. In the 1990s, the Sahel region was referred to by Christian mission bodies as 'the zone of encounter'. This suggested that battle-lines were drawn between Christians and Muslims. The line was not drawn in the sand but in the air: some sort of invisible fault-line exists in the spiritual realm over that area like a spiritual principality that feeds the violent clashes from Nigeria through Sudan to Somaliland.

This line of friction is the tenth degree latitude on the map, the bottom line of the 10/40 Window. However, it is important to add that the violence is not simply between Christians and Muslims; the underlying issue is the deeply entrenched tribalism that also happens to follow the lines of religious demarcation and even within Christian tribes that have a split allegiance to one Christian denomination or another.

The reason for this goes back a century to when Christian missions first entered Africa. The tribal groups were shared out among different missions who worked in their allotted areas. In good faith, each mission reproduced their denomination with which the local tribes became identified. Sadly, denominationalism inadvertently became added to the existing tribal and racial identity. In some cases this has become the trigger for periodic violence and even killings among fellow Christians. This situation is something which concerns mission groups working in the region today.

The evangelist Reinhard Bonnke and his team had to be escorted out of Nigeria as Muslim rioters surrounded their hotel. Eight people were killed in the protests, which were provoked by plans for a series of Christian meetings where the sick would be prayed for in the northern city of Kano. The official reason for the riots was that young Muslim men reacted to the idea that the power of God could be transferred to a man who could heal the sick. The word on the street was that the authorities had refused a similar Muslim rally with a visiting speaker but had allowed the Christians to have such a meeting.

I learned that the inter-tribal problems were usually rooted in the politics of tribalism which expressed itself through religious allegiance. On one occasion I was shopping for cloth in the city of Jos, the capital of Plateau State. When I found some cloth I liked, I noticed it had the Islamic crescent moon (*ḥillel*) woven into it. I reluctantly handed it back to the assistant and said, 'I'm sorry I can't wear this because I support the other team.' We both paused then fell about laughing. Both of us understood what the point was without another word being said. 'Islam' and 'Christianity' do actually function as a social marker as, for instance, Protestant and Catholic do in Northern Ireland. I also learned that the unrest in Nigeria tended to be driven (at least on the Muslim side) by a few corrupt and power-hungry men who wanted absolute control and were using Islam as the convenient ideology and its assertive potential as a useful tool to get power.

Another example of the political nature of Islam is the violence of Sudan where the Khartoum government practice a 'scorched earth' policy of genocide against the southern 'Christian' tribes. I saw the bullet-ridden and blood-spattered walls of burnt-out buildings in the abandoned villages; the spent chemical canisters labelled in Arabic as originating in Iraq (Saddam's weapons of mass destruction?) and the traumatized, starving children. I also saw the dazed and hopeless faces of raped women; the maimed bodies of men who had survived prison and torture because they were Christian. I also saw the pain on the faces of the widows of martyred men.

Such inter-communal violence is a difficult context in which to model grace to anyone. I found it especially hard because I suffered from a lack of credibility. Whatever I said or did to try and help church leaders, we all knew that I would be boarding a plane soon. It had been so different for me back in Egypt in the 1980s. When President Sadat was assassinated and Libya threatened to invade, I was very much one of the local believers and as such I held much more credibility: everyone knew that I intended to face it through with them.

I found that both secular and Christian media under-report the positive stories that come out of such trouble-spots. Action Partners' staff on the ground in Nigeria would tell me how Muslims and Christians alike were hiding one another in their homes in order to protect each other from the Muslim and Christian mobs.

I felt privileged to play a small part in the process of attitude change among African Christians with regard to their Muslim neighbours. I also needed to reassure African Christians that, contrary to the claims they were hearing via the Muslim-influenced Hausa Section of the BBC World Service, Islam was not taking over in Britain. I complained strenuously to the BBC about this propagandist use of their radio programming and got an apology from them.

I also held seminars in which I urged denominational leaders to train and appoint African Christian specialists in Islamics to lecturing positions in African theological colleges. In one conference we estimated that the leaders present held influence in constituencies that, when put together, numbered about twelve million members. I was delighted that the appointment of such Islamic specialists to colleges began to happen in a small way. It will be a long process for the African church but Islam is slowly coming onto its agenda. For the African church, the issue is Christian/Muslim tribal proximity, while in the West it is multi-cultural communities. In some ways the African church may be ahead of the British church in considering these things.

Christian/Muslim interface in Britain

As I continued in my role as a mission leader, I was increasingly drawn towards the situation in the UK and the need for confident yet humble cross-cultural witness to British Muslims. As an itinerant visitor to many local churches I could see that, on the whole, the British church had been faithful in sending workers to Muslim lands across the globe but was not so good at responding to Muslims who were living across the road.

I became aware of the fact that the task of interacting with British Muslim communities is made doubly difficult because of the cultural strength of the Muslim community. The Muslim perceives the security and support of the social network as being a direct benefit of Islam. This is only indirectly true because this holistic support is as much to do with these eastern cultures themselves. They were like this long before Islam arrived. Muslim cultures have traditionally provided so much for the individuals in them that Muslims are less available for friendship with anyone outside their close-knit circle – except as an outside confidante. As a result, the extended family may be the only social network that many Muslims know. The opposite is true for most westerners who are free to relate more widely with whoever they wish.

If anything, the tight-knit nature of Muslim communities is getting even tighter as they turn in on themselves for support. Analyst Patrick Sookhdeo warns that this looks set to strengthen still further until the day when British Muslims form a 'state within a state'. He believes this will happen as Muslim clerics who believe in concentration, not integration, influence the political agenda until they control these areas by *shari'a* law, not common law. According to Sookdheo, such clerics are already pressing for the 'right' to practise *shari'a* and see any resistance as racist and 'Islamophobic'.[3]

A survey conducted for the *Telegraph* newspaper found that four out of ten British Muslims already want to see *shari'a* law enforced in areas of Britain with large Muslim populations. In response to this, the Chief Executive of the Commission for Racial Equality, Trevor Phillips, said publicly that 'Britain must have one set of laws decided by Parliament and anyone who wants something different (i.e. such as *shari'a* law) has the option of living somewhere else'.[4]

In the UK, Muslims still do not appreciate that the West is only culturally Christian and that in Britain practising Christians are a minority, like themselves. Both are endeavouring to live for God in a society which is both religiously pluralist and yet largely secular – at the same time. In this respect Christians and Muslims have not yet found one another to be the potential allies (on certain issues) that they could be. I found that both groups are trying to live counter-cultural lives in a secular environment with hardly any reference to one another. I came to see the need for regular interaction groups to be set up between Christians and Muslims all over the UK, Europe and the West.

Many Muslims are now second, third and even fourth generation Britons who hold British passports. It is too late to unscramble the egg of immigration. Britain has become a truly multi-cultural place. However, what would it take for Britain to become genuinely multi-cultural? Over a decade later, this is still a vexed question after words have been bandied about such as 'integration' and the more idealistic notion of 'assimilation'. Neither have been properly achieved and if anything we are further away from either of them now than then.

I have always been able to identify with British immigrants because I too, am a son of an Afro-Caribbean economic migrant. Many Muslims of my age are as British as me. I, like the second and third generations of Muslims, do not have any ties to my father's country of origin. We have nowhere else to go. We are British.

Muslim concerns

My role as an itinerant mission speaker in Britain, Canada, Australia and New Zealand was influenced by the challenge of helping western Christians to come to terms with the fact that many of them have an attitude problem towards the Muslim. Wherever I have gone, I always urged people not to view Muslims as 'the enemy within' and to realize that in some respects it is the West itself that is 'the enemy'. This was easier said than done, though. I was often surprised at the number of intelligent westerners who failed to realize that the influence of the West in the Muslim world was perceived as a negative thing by most Muslims. The need to get some clarity and balance on this issue featured prominently on my agenda. I would be invited to churches to promote mission but would end up answering a barrage of questions about Muslims. While pleased that people were noticing Muslims more, I would also break the news that Muslims feel the way they do about the West not in order to be awkward but because they were grappling with some significant issues to which the West at times seems oblivious. These include:

Globalization

Muslims firstly react to what they see as western commercial, as well as cultural, domination. We live in a globalized world that is largely driven by the West and in which the Muslim world has had little part and cannot compete. Regardless of whether or not the Muslim world is simply jealous of the goodies possessed by the West, they tend to view the situation as unfair, unrighteous in terms of morality and unhelpful in terms of international relations.

Another problem with globalization is that the West is seen as exporting a secularist worldview that is conveyed through Hollywood, satellite TV and the internet. When I lived in the Middle East, I was disappointed to find soap operas like *Dallas* being screened on prime-time terrestrial TV. In Egypt, I regularly fielded questions about western lifestyle from Muslims who assumed Dallas was typical. I was recently in Tunisia and was saddened to find that *Big Brother* was being received there. I can understand Muslims reacting to this sort of material because, as a Christian, I join Muslims in asking, 'Is this the sort of society we want anywhere?'

Western foreign policy

Perhaps most significantly, I would have to explain to Christians in the late 1990s how many Muslims take an extremely negative view of western foreign policy. This is an issue that has got worse since the 1990s. I would find myself pointing out that Muslims see western society as having extremely weak spiritual and moral credentials. As a result, Muslims are astonished that such countries should assume the right to interfere in the affairs of Muslim countries, which they see as possessing stronger spiritual and moral values.

Please balance what I am about to say with the fact that I am as pro-Jewish as I am pro-Muslim. I used to visit Israel regularly through the 1980s because I was a next door neighbour in Egypt. I knew enriching friendships with Jews, one of whom said to me, 'You and I have two things in common – you are black and I am a Jew and we are both following Christ.' I am not ignorant of the biblical material about the Jewish 'favoured nation status'. I do not dispute this but I do take issue with some people about its implications today. With the above proviso, allow me to describe western foreign policy from the Muslim point of view.

The Sykes-Picot Agreement
To Muslims, the root of the current Middle Eastern problem goes back to the privately crafted Sykes-Picot Agreement of May 1916. This was only intended to be a provisional agreement but it effectively carved up the best

bits of the Middle Eastern part of the Ottoman Empire and put them under British and French control while leaving the sparsely populated desert areas as autonomous Arab sheikhdoms. Oil was later discovered in the desert in huge quantities which contributed to a resurgence of Arab confidence in the region. To the Arab mind western nations were dishonest when they promised land that was not theirs in return for co-operation.

A recent knock-on effect of the Sykes-Picot Agreement was the first Gulf War in 1991. Underlying that conflict was Saddam Hussein's belief in a historic claim to Kuwaiti territory which he understood to be part of what we now know as Iraq. Of course in 1916 neither Iraq nor Kuwait existed, as such. These and other Middle Eastern nations came into being when lines were arbitrarily drawn in the sand by British and French politicians.

It took the Russian Revolution in 1917 to bring to light what had been going on behind closed doors. The Tsar's foreign ministry was ransacked by Bolsheviks and the small print of the Sykes-Picot Agreement was discovered and divulged to Turkey, who had sided with Germany against Britain and France. Turkey informed the Arabs of what became seen as 'treachery against the Muslim peoples of the Ottoman Empire on the part of the Christian powers of Europe'.[5]

The Jewish State of Israel

The establishment of the State of Israel has been deeply divisive. The ongoing conflict which has ensued suggests that the West's actions were not in the best interests of either the Jews or the Palestinians and have been unfair to both. The latest chapter in the complex history of the Holy Land began in the early part of the twentieth century when only twenty-five thousand Jews lived in what was then called Palestine. The majority Palestinian population are an Arabized people who migrated from the eastern islands of the Mediterranean and who have been inhabitants of the so-called Holy Land for centuries.

The vision of a homeland for the Jews was first proposed by Theodore Herzl in 1897 when the first Zionist Congress was held in Basel, Switzerland. The idea took shape in the mind of Jews worldwide during a period of persecution of Jews in Russia and Germany. Thousands began arriving in Palestine where they bought land and property from absentee Arab landlords and integrated with Palestinian neighbours.

In 1916 Arthur Balfour, who was sympathetic to the Jewish cause, became British Foreign Minister. He persuaded the British government to support the Jews in the knowledge that this would bode well for British/American relations at a time when Britain was increasingly likely to need America as an ally. Balfour initiated what became known as the Balfour Declaration which, although falling short of supporting a Jewish State, did declare Britain's support for some sort of 'Jewish homeland' in Palestine, with the proviso that the rights of non-Jews would be safeguarded.

As the Jewish population began to dominate in Palestine, tensions rose and in 1929 sixty Jews were killed during riots in Hebron. A siege mentality developed among Jews who remembered the persecutions they had fled from. Boatloads of Jews began arriving as the Nazi holocaust got underway. By the outbreak of the Second World War, there were around one hundred thousand Jews in Palestine. The fragile balance of populations there was lost amid violent Jewish/Palestinian clashes. At one point British troops even tried to stop the influx of holocaust survivors at Palestine's ports. The Jews vowed that genocide would never happen again – certainly not in Palestine. The inevitable Jewish siege mentality was a result of the constant threat of extermination. This led to them taking up arms as a way of life.

In 1947 Britain handed Palestine over to the United Nations. The State of Israel was declared on 14 May 1948 and President Truman of the United States immediately gave it formal recognition. Ongoing conflict has followed that decision, off and on, till this day. (For a fuller description of the wars that have followed, see the Appendix).

Britain cannot be blamed for the conflict of the past sixty years, but it can be blamed for the political actions that included promising land to the Jewish immigrants that it did not own and which was not vacant. The actions of western governments in the lead-up to the establishment of the State of Israel forced the Jewish government into a defensive position against the Palestinians, who they feel they need to repress in the battle for survival. On the other hand elements in the Palestinian community have battled for their rights as they see them. This has turned them into terrorists or freedom fighters – depending on your point of view. There is sufficient similarity between the struggles of the Palestinians and that of the IRA to draw attention to this parallel in the hope that it may help us grasp the struggle for land and political autonomy that has been common to both. The Israeli/Palestinian conflict has as much to do with Islam as the Northern Ireland conflict has to do with Christianity.

The Palestinians may have become pawns in a chess game. As Muslims they are useful to Islamic countries that are intent on making political capital in the hope of regaining Jerusalem as an Islamic city. Little help for Palestinians seems to come from the wealthy Gulf States other than money to build yet more mosques in the Palestinian territories. Meanwhile the Palestinians face financial dependency on western aid to survive. The Palestinians have also been affected by the in-fighting, internal corruption and the misappropriation of funds by both the PLO and Fatah. This helped Hamas win victory at the polls in 2005.

Several in the Palestinian leadership have made the familiar threat to force all Israeli Jews out of Israel and into the sea. However, less well known is the fact that this sentiment is not unique to the PLO or Hamas. It originated with men like Joseph Weitz, director of the Jewish National Land Fund in 1940, who said of the Palestinians, 'It must be clear that there is no room for both peoples in this country. If Arabs stay, the country will remain narrow and miserable. The only solution is Israel without Arabs. There is no room for compromise on this point'.[6] David Ben-Gurion, Israel's first Prime Minister also said 'We will expel the Arabs and take their place'[8]; so the sentiment of expulsion of the other is mutual.

In the early days of the State of Israel a policy of ethnic cleansing was undertaken by Jewish military brigades such as the Irgun (led by Menachem Begin), the Stern Gang (led by Yizhak Shamir) and the Haganah and is now being uncovered by historians.[8] As a resident in the Middle East and a frequent visitor to Israel, I struggled with the conditions in which displaced Palestinians live in the refugee camps around the country and in Jordan. On the other hand, the violence of the Palestine Liberation Organization and the Palestinian Islamist groups, such as Hamas, is an unrighteous response to the unrighteous actions of the Jewish military.

Film-maker Steven Spielberg's film *Munich* (February 2006) was a controversial attempt to portray the vicious cruelty of the Palestinian attacks on Israeli athletes at the Munich Olympics. The film also tries to illustrate the

ruthless revenge of the Israeli secret services as they
assassinated all those suspected of being part of that plot.
However, the added salt in the wound (from the Muslim
viewpoint) is the UN's lack of even-handedness and an
apparent political bias towards the State of Israel
particularly by the American administration. While some
people fall prey to conspiracy theories in this area, it is
nevertheless difficult to determine the extent to which
American interest groups, such as the wealthy and
influential Jewish lobby, affect US support.

> With such a history of persecution, the state of Israel is of
> great importance to Jews today. If persecution should ever
> break out again they have a refuge, a homeland. This is why
> many peace-loving, prosperous Jews are willing to fight for
> Israel.[9]

We should also not forget the large and pro-Israel
Evangelical right-wing constituency, which has influence
in America.

Uncomprehending Muslims resent the influence of
some prominent western Christians, such as Franklin
Graham and Pat Robertson, who have made inflamma-
tory public statements on Christian TV and in the press
about Muslims and the Israeli/Palestinian situation
regardless of whether or not they are qualified to do so.
This gives Muslims the impression that all western
Christians uncritically endorse whatever the Israeli
administration does.

I have already suggested that the problem for many
western Christians is the tendency to confuse the biblical
or prophetic Israel with the reality of the modern State
of Israel. The biblical prophets (and a growing number
of Israeli Jews) protest strongly about the aspects of
injustice, human rights abuse and secular values, all

of which are part of life in modern Israel. I feel for the fair-minded Jews who lament some of the things that are going on in the country. Christians would be more use if they invested time praying for Israel rather than delving into prophetic speculation. The sovereign God is working out his purpose for both Jewish and Palestinian people, as well as the land. As Christians we need to remain firmly on the side of the God of the Bible and pray for biblical justice and righteousness in the modern State of Israel.

The Suez crisis
Another issue that has led to Muslim disillusionment with the West was the Suez crisis and its aftermath. In the 1950s, Gamal Abdul Nasser, the leader of Egypt, developed the 'pan-Arab' vision of uniting Egypt with several other Arabic speaking states in a nationalistic confederacy which could stand up to the West. This was a threat to Britain's colonial interests in Egypt as well as to Saudi Arabia's privileged position as the chief supplier of oil in the region. Consequently, a serious amount of western money was poured into the bank accounts of the first Muslim Brotherhood in Egypt, which was founded by Sayed Al-Qutb. The West's aim was to bring Nasser's regime down.[10]

Qutb's writings became an early influence on the young Osama Bin Laden. In a similar way, the first corporate sponsor of Al-Qaeda was, strictly speaking, America. It was the US administration that originally equipped the Taliban with American-supplied arms that enabled them to fight as *mujahideen* to oust the Russians from Afghanistan. At the time, the term 'Mujahideen' was naïvely understood in the West to be a quaint Islamic term for freedom fighters. Taliban leaders were duly invited to Washington as VIPs. This is a point not missed by the controversial Michael Moore documentary film *Fahrenheit 9/11*.[11] This arrangement suited both US foreign policy and the Taliban's goal of resisting the attempted annexation of Afghanistan by Moscow.

After the defeat of the Russians, the US dropped the Taliban, who started to turn against America. They now recognized the social problems of their own society and resented the fact that their 'friends' in Washington were not interested in helping them to reconstruct Afghanistan – only that they did not become the latest satellite of the Russian Federation. Out of this disillusionment, Al-Qaeda emerged under the leadership of Osama Bin Laden, an enigmatic Saudi Arabian of Yemeni extraction who left the Gulf to stand with his Afghani brothers to defend the interests of Islam in Central Asia. America thus became the new target for *jihadic* struggle in an attempt to resist the perceived western interference in the East, and the wrongs done in Muslim lands.

Afghanistan
Post 9/11, the Taliban's fundamentalist domination of Afghanistan became the new focus of Washington's War on Terror. America did return its attention to Afghanistan; in order to oust the Taliban themselves. Washington now called them terrorists. The West was surprised when the Taliban refused to give up Bin Laden who was hiding among them as their guest. The message from Capitol Hill and Westminster began to change. Now Islam was required to be not a religion of liberation to fight oppression, but a religion of peace. Western Muslims were now required to be loyal citizens who integrated well and affirmed western values. Analyst Anthony McRoy suggests that

If Britain and America had not developed this pattern of 'interference' in the Middle East at several points in their histories, secular nationalism might now be the unchallenged popular ideology from Morocco to Iran and the position of Christian minorities more secure. Instead, Western policy laid the foundations for Khomeini and Al-Qaeda.[12]

This is the irony of the situation as appreciated by the more observant Muslims in both East and West. This history of interference in Muslim lands is an issue for many Muslims who wonder if western governments can ever be trusted. In this instance, the West is in need of the East's grace.

Christian concerns

On my travels around Britain I noticed that Christians are often unable to include the word 'grace' and 'Muslim' in the same sentence. One reason for this is the fact that they feel threatened by the rising birth-rate amongst Muslims. The Muslim population growth is because of high birth-rates and not because of conversion, as is sometimes claimed. This is an issue in European countries such as France and Holland where indigenous families are having far fewer children. By 2030 both these countries will have Muslim majority populations if the present birth-rates continue.[13] However, in order to keep things in perspective we must remember that there are twice as many people in the world who claim a Christian allegiance. In fact there are almost as many Catholics in the world as Muslims. This may be little comfort to people who feel swamped by Muslims but it is a fact that must be factored into the equation when talking about the knotty immigration problems facing some European countries. Writer Anne Lamott has said, 'We can safely assume we have created a God in our own image when it turns out that even He hates all the same people we do.'[14]

Surely the answer to this is for Christians to discover grace, grace and more grace. Philip Yancey observed how in the gospels Jesus was so attractive. People fled *towards* him for refuge; including morally fallen prostitutes, desperately sick people, the socially excluded poor and even a culturally and religiously marginalized Samaritan. Yancey asks why the same types of people no longer feel welcome among his followers today.[15] This is a good question.

I came to the conclusion that it is the politician, not the ordinary Christian, who needs to know the alarming things that some Muslims get up to. The primary thing for the Christian is that they know how to relate to Muslims rather than becoming so alarmed that they run in the opposite direction. There seemed nothing else for it. The situation needed some sort of itinerant adviser to help Christians find their bearings. I had no idea that such a person was going to be me.

Will the real enemy please stand up?'

While Christians were becoming increasingly concerned about the Muslim presence in Britain, I became more aware of the irony that the real enemy is not the Muslims at all but the politically correct secularism that provides a platform for the Islamizing of some aspects of British life. One Muslim described secularism as 'a new religion in itself; a total negation of God'.[16] I began to identify secularism as the subtle and all-pervasive influence that is eating away at the vitals of Judeo-Christian values. If I wanted to be paranoid, secularism seems to be a far more worthy candidate for the position of hidden enemy than Islam.

I described the effects of this corrosive influence on British society as 'aggressive secularism'. I found myself being slightly amused by the fact that most Muslims are as concerned as Christians about the secular values that are being aggressively enforced in our society. Here are some examples . . .

- A retired Christian couple Joe and Helen Roberts were interrogated for eighty minutes by police who were called in by the local council in Fleetwood, Blackpool. The Roberts had complained to the council about its gay rights policies and were being accused of homophobia. The Roberts also asked if they could display Christian literature next to gay rights material in public places and were refused because 'it may offend homosexuals'.[17]
- All Saints Anglican Church High Wycombe was told by the local authority that it could not display a poster advertizing a Christmas Carol Service on a public library noticeboard because it might 'offend people of other religions'.[19]
- A church was taken to court for refusing to employ a practising homosexual person in their office in line with EU legislation on equal employment opportunities. Another church faced a court case when they refused to allow a male transgender person to use the ladies' toilets and join a ladies' meeting.[18]
- St Anthony's Primary School in Boardsley Green, Birmingham, was asked by the local authority to remove the 'Saint' from their name in order to 'reflect the multi-cultural nature of the area and avoid marginalizing ethnic minorities'. Muslim Councillor Mahmoud

resisted the move saying, 'It is political correctness gone too far. The aim of multiculturalism is not to obliterate the Christian roots of Britain.'[20]

- Sections of the Muslim community stood with secularists like actor Rowan Atkinson (who plays Mr Bean), humanists and Evangelical Christians to oppose the Incitement to Religious Hatred Bill. Muslims said 'If this government will not fight for faith in national life – we will'.[21]

- The committed Catholic Euro-politician Rocco Buttiglione was nominated as European Commissioner designate but was dramatically ousted on the grounds that his beliefs were 'incompatible with the European Parliament'. Buttiglione believes Europe is becoming as totalitarian as the former Communist states. He believes that a truly free Europe is one in which homosexuals are free to do what they like as long as others are also just as free to claim that what they do is wrong.

- A male colleague of mine serving as a volunteer on a personnel support group of a Christian mission was sacked by a local authority for refusing (on religious grounds) to follow a guideline which promoted same-sex relationships.

- A Christian doctor friend of mine was asked to leave a post as a locum after a complaint by a woman who had previously suffered from a severe sexually transmitted disease. She took exception because the doctor had suggested that she rethink her lifestyle because she was about to start a new relationship with a man whose sexual history she knew little about.

- A senior social worker told me how she was nearly sacked for refusing to affirm the lifestyle of a trans-sexual person who was intent on multiple relation-ships. It took her seniority and skill to hang on to her job.

- BBC Radio 4 News reported moves to discard the name 'Red Cross' in favour of 'Red Diamond'.

Political correspondent Daniel Johnson suggests that what he calls 'secular fundamentalism' is 'as much of an internal threat to our civilization as the external one of religious fundamentalism'. Johnson cites the British Conservative MP Oliver Letwin (a Jewish atheist) who has said

> Our national symbols are inseparable from Christianity. There is no Crescent or Star of David nor any other religious symbol but the Cross. In ten years time, if it is still legal to proclaim Jesus Christ as the only way to heaven, a proposition from which I dissent, I will wish to preserve the right of others to utter it.[22]

The politically correct philosophy has grown partly out of a sense of post-colonial guilt, which has made some former colonial nations such as Britain sensitive to the need for fairness. As a black person, I appreciate this. However, this has become driven by secular extremists to the point of silliness – hence the ban on the use of words like 'blackboard' (which is not offensive to black people anyway) in favour of 'chalkboard'. This secularist agenda has driven political correctness to the point where society is intolerant of anything that does not comply with it.

Canadian journalist George Jonas commented on how western countries are 'exporting freedom while importing intolerance'.

> Far from assimilating newcomers or trading partners into Western ways of freedom under the law, we're continually redefining our traditions to accommodate the touchy moods of Eastern despotisms that combine lawlessness with

religious and political sensitivity. We haven't strengthened individual liberties in other regions nearly as much as we've reduced them at home. Today, we're less free to speak, associate, do business, choose pastimes or lifestyles than we were fifty years ago. While Tripoli is no closer to Ottawa than it was in 1950, Ottawa is getting closer to Tripoli.[23]

It is aggressive secularism, not Islam, that wants the demise of Christianity in Britain. Muslims have made it clear to me that, contrary to the claims of the politically correct gurus who use Muslims as leverage for their secular agenda, many Muslims wish that Britain was more Christian, not less.

The itinerant mission promoter role became the preparation for the next phase that I was about to embark on. Although I did not realize it at the time, it was going to take a tragedy to release me from mission leadership. The tragedy was to catapult me into a new sphere of life and work that would take me to various parts of the world.

Notes

1. S. Green (Ed.), *Britain in Sin* (Sutton: Christian Voice – National Statistical Report, 1998).
2. *Interface*, the magazine of Action Partners Ministries, Issue No.8 2005.
3. Alasdair Palmer, News Review & Comment (*Sunday Telegraph* 19 February 2006), p15.
4. Steve Doughty, *Daily Mail* (27 February 2006), p2.
5. Peter Mansfield, *The Arabs* (Harmondsworth: Penguin Books, 1976), p199.
6. T. M. McAleavy, *The Arab-Israeli Conflict* (Cambridge: Cambridge University Press, 1998), p22.
7. Gary Burge, *Whose Land? Whose Promise?* (Paternoster Press, 2003), p37.

8. Gary Burge, *Whose Land? Whose Promise?* (Pilgrim Press, 2003), p39.

9. Martin Goldsmith & Rosemary Harley, *Who is my Neighbour? – World faiths, understanding and communicating* (Carlisle: Authentic Lifestyle/OMF Publishing, 1988), p46.

10. Said Aburish, *Nasser: The Last Arab* (London: Duckworth, 2004), p257.

11. Michael Moore, *Fahrenheit 9/11 – Controversy . . . What controversy?* (Optimum HomeEntertainment, 2004).

12. A. McRoy, 'Did the West cause the rise of Islam?' (*Evangelicals Now*, July 2005), p15.

13. Barbara Amiel, Is France on the way to becoming an Islamic state? (*Daily Telegraph*, 26 January 2004);
Brian Moynehan, 'Putting the fear of God into Holland', (*The Sunday Times Magazine*, 27 February 2005), p34-42.

14. Anne Lamott, *Travelling Mercies – some thoughts on faith* (Wilmington NC: Anchor, 2000).

15. Philip Yancey, *What's so amazing about grace?* (London: Harper Collins, 1997), p11.

16. *Daily Telegraph* (20 September 2003), p23.

17. *Dispatches* (BBC Channel 4, Monday 27 February 2006), also reported in the *Daily Mail*, 23 December 2005; also in *Update*, the UK Newsletter of the Christian Institute (Issue 7 Spring 2006), p9.

18. The Christian Institute, PO Box 1, Newcastle upon Tyne, NE7 7EF. Tel: 0191 282 5664, email:info@christian.org.uk, www.christian.org.uk.

19. Stewart Payne article, 'The day that Christmas carols fell foul of the PC brigade' (*Daily Telegraph*, Friday 12 December 2003).

20. Item on BBC1 West Midlands local news, December 27 2005.

21. J. Petre, N. Tweedie & B. Carlin, 'Muslims join plea to reject new religious hatred laws' (*Daily Telegraph*, 5 February 2006), p10.

22. Daniel Johnson, 'The threat of secular fundamentalism' (*Daily Telegraph*, 16 April 2003).

23. George Jonas, 'Exporting freedom, importing intolerance' (*Canadian National Post*, 27 December 2004).

Interlude

Grace seeking Muslims

'Osama Bin Laden is responsible for more Muslims following Jesus than anyone else alive today'
Patrick Johnstone

Patrick Johnstone is the founding author of *Operation World*.[1] His claim is backed up by his years of research. The claim is made because the atrocities that are being committed by radical Islamists seem to be backfiring on them. By that I mean that while Islamists are inflicting judgement on non-Muslims for their secular materialism, moderate Muslims see what is being done in the name of Islam and are saying to themselves, 'If this is the truest expression of Islam, I don't want it.' Some such moderates are choosing to find other ways of submitting to God; including the option of turning away from the 'way of the Prophet' (i.e. Muhammad) and instead following Islam's second most prominent prophet – *'isa al-masih* (Jesus Christ).

This fact is a challenge to the many Christians who have told me over the years that 'Muslims will change their religion only when leopards change their spots.'

Evidence now shows that Muslims can and are following Jesus. My encounter with Ahmad and others in the early 1980s proved to be just the tip of an iceberg. This claim is supported by analysts such as David Garrison. He goes even further, saying that 'More Muslims have come to Christ in the past two decades than at any other point in history'.[2]

I am one of a minority who have been calling for Christians to approach Muslims with love. I appreciate the moral support of Brother Andrew, who would visit when I lived in Egypt. Since then he has gone on record as saying that 'We must start spelling Islam "I Sincerely Love All Muslims." We need to take time to get to know Muslims and show them real love'.[3]

Taking this stance does not mean we have to become politically naïve about the agenda of radical Muslims. I have always been concerned about the potential of such radicals especially when they become politically subversive or organize themselves into the networks that are sympathetic to Al-Qaeda's vision. The Christian response to this sort of Muslim is the power-encounter which comes by concerted intercessory prayer. However, the Muslims who are turning to Christ are not from the radical core but the moderate fringe. These are the ones I call 'ordinary' Muslims. My optimism for Muslims comes not from the popular lack of understanding that is usually based on shallow news coverage, but from first-hand experience of living and travelling in the Muslim world. It is my personal knowledge of Muslims, both radical and ordinary ones, that has brought me to the place where the love of God can come in when needed and dissipate fear. The Bible is clear that love and fear cannot co-exist (1 Jn. 4:18). As a result, my instinctive reaction to Muslims is no longer one of fear or anger but compassion.

I try to ignore the sense of isolation I feel among western Christians because I know that the small number of us who believe that Muslims will follow Jesus Christ is growing. Destructive fear is turning into constructive prayer. This is a trend that has been paralleled over the past twenty-five years by a marked increase in the activity of God's Spirit among Muslims around the world. Take, for instance, a Pakistani-born British Muslim woman who became a follower of Jesus in Leicester. She told me that when she visits her extended family in her Pakistani home town, she finds more Muslims following Jesus there than she does in the UK. Logic says this should be the other way around but these are the upside-down ways of God. The following statistics are based on the research of Reverend Dr David Barrett.[4]

God's sovereign activity in his world

- In 1900 there were only eight million Christians in Africa. As colonial rule ended in the 1960s the church went into explosive growth. In the last thirty-five years, the church has trebled to a staggering 390 million. Today there are more Nigerian Anglicans than in the 'mixed-bag' of Britain, Europe and the USA combined.

   The African church is set to increase by another two hundred million by the year 2020.
- During the 1970s the South American church began to experience revival until the conversion rate in places such as the Amazonas region of Northern Brazil became five times the birth rate for several years. The evangelicals of South America have grown from 250,000 in 1900 to sixty million today.

- During the 1980s the South East Asian church saw steady increase. A hundred years ago there was not a single church in Seoul City, South Korea. Today the city is home to seven of the world's ten largest churches, including David Cho Yonggi's Yehoida Full Gospel Church, with a membership of two hundred and fifty thousand. Today, one in three South Koreans is a follower of Jesus.
- Seven per cent of the eight million contracted overseas Philippino workers are evangelical Christians. The Philippino church has set a target of sending out two hundred thousand vocational or 'tent maker' missionaries by the year 2010.
- In Singapore there is one missionary sent out for every one thousand church members, possibly the highest percentage in the world.
- When the Berlin Wall came down, the church in the communist world started to grow. Today Ukraine has a church-planting movement through which hundreds of new churches have come into existence.
- The Chinese government admits to an underground church of twenty million while the underground church networks say that the number is nearer one hundred million. This figure outnumbers the Chinese Communist Party membership of seventy million.[5]
- What will we see in the next twenty years? While many British Christians long for a visitation in Europe, it seems that the early twenty-first century is likely to be a time for the Muslim world in which hundreds of thousands of Muslims choose to follow Jesus Christ.
- In one area of India, up to fifty thousand Muslims are following Jesus.
- Hundreds of thousands of Muslims are choosing to follow Jesus in countries such as Kazakhstan, Azerbaijan, Bangladesh, Bulgaria, Egypt, Indonesia, Jordan, Iran, Palestine, Iraq, Turkey and across North Africa.

- In an interview on Al-Jazeera TV, Sheikh Ahmad Al-Qataani, a Libyan Islamic cleric, claimed that hundreds of Muslims were turning to Christ every day in his country. This is an exaggeration, possibly aimed at creating a negative reaction. Iranian cleric Hassan Mohammadi of the Ministry of Education has also stated publicly that an estimated fifty Iranian young people are turning to Christ every day, including the children of mullahs and government ministers.[6] God is at work and some Muslim leaders know it.

It is time for the western church to make a connection between the patient 'tilling of hard ground' over the centuries and the present movements of Muslims to Christ. New technology is also reaching the once isolated areas to reap a harvest that was faithfully sown during the previous years; for example radio, satellite TV, the internet, CD Rom and DVD. Sources in the Gulf report seeing the DVD of the Mel Gibson film *The Passion of the Christ* selling out of the boots of cars in areas where there were no cinemas because of the strict Wahabi Islamic laws. The Spirit of God is also working through dreams, visions, healing and deliverance. Jesus is regularly appearing to Muslims in various places. Here are some examples.

- A group of Nigerian Muslims saw Jesus as they were performing the *hajj* pilgrimage at the *ka'aba* (the black cube) in the heart of Mecca.
- Jesus told a string of individual Gulf Arabs the exact name and address of a Christian bookshop in a neighbouring Middle Eastern country where they could buy the Bible. The shop owner told me that one of them walked in and pointed to a picture of Jesus on the wall and said, 'He told me where I could buy the *injil* (Gospel).'

- Minaz Somani is from the *isma'ili* group within Islam, and had his marriage blessed by its spiritual leader, the Agha Khan. Minaz owns the franchise of a luxury car dealership in the north of England. One day in 1999 while he was at home, a light, similar to a photographic flash gun, came into the room. The face of Jesus appeared in the light and he spoke to Minaz for about ten minutes. During this time Minaz felt the love of God enter his body, cleanse him internally and heal him. He began to follow Jesus that day and soon afterwards his wife joined him. They now run an outreach to others.

- Jesus appeared simultaneously to an Islamic cleric in the Middle East and at the foot of the bed of his dangerously ill daughter in Germany. As Jesus told the cleric he was healing the girl, she was instantly cured in a German hospital. When the sheikh received confirmation by phone of the miraculous healing, he left the country with his family in order to follow Jesus.

- One of the earliest books written about a follower of Jesus from Muslim background was the autobiography called *I Dared to Call Him Father*.[7] This is the story of Bilquis Sheikh, a high-born wealthy Pakistani woman who found her way to Christ. Her journey began when she had a vision of Yehia (John the Baptist) from the Qur'an. He was standing at a crossroads and beckoning to her. She asked the meaning of the vision from a Christian missionary, who told her that John's role was to point people to Christ. She eventually discovered that God was her Father and that this may be the missing hundredth Name of God in the 'Ninety-Nine Beautiful Names of God' in Islam.[8]

- I was informed by a non-Christian journalist in London that Bangladeshis in the high-rise flats of the East End have been having visitations from Jesus and angels for some time. This has been going on in parallel with significant numbers of conversions in Bangladesh.

- Sources in Iran say that since the Iranian Revolution in 1979, tens of thousands of Iranian Shi'ite Muslims are following Jesus Christ inside Iran, in spite of sporadic persecution. Thousands more Iranians around the world are following Jesus.
- One North African nation has one of the fastest church-growth movements in the Muslim world. There are an estimated 50-80,000 Muslims who are following Jesus and an estimated fifty home fellowships are being set up every year. One observer said the 'awakening' in this region looks more like the Book of Acts. Believers are meeting in homes daily in spite of opposition. They also experience dreams, visions and healings. Even former terrorists and Islamic sorcerers are now following Jesus.[9]
- As I write, I have a photo on my desk of me and a Central Asian Muslim man called Tahir. The picture was taken in 2003 at a location in the former Soviet Union where I helped set up an annual training course to prepare people to take the Gospel to the Muslims of the Central Asian Republics. These are the 'istan' nations, such as Tajikistan and Uzbekistan.

Tahir is built like a wrestler. Only his broad smile reassures you that he is not going to beat you up. For most of his life, Tahir had little reason to smile because his difficult circumstances caused him to suffer prolonged, severe bouts of depression. He took drugs in order to mask the pain. He felt condemned because he was not a good Muslim. In his late twenties, he tried to take his life by slashing his wrists and attempting to disembowel himself. As he began to lose consciousness in a pool of blood, Tahir cried out to God for help. Jesus appeared to him and told him he would heal his body, cleanse his soul and make him a witness to others. He was discovered and taken to hospital.

The Arabic word *tâhir* means 'pure' or 'fresh'. This is a fitting name for a Muslim who has received a 'pure' heart and newness of life in Christ. Today Tahir reaches out to his own people. He showed me the gruesome scarring on his abdomen that he will carry for life.

- One Christian organization reports that over five hundred Muslims are visiting its Arabic website each month to enquire about Jesus. It is also reported that over the past ten years a thousand home fellowships of believers from Muslim backgrounds have been set up across the Middle East.

- A survey showed that 20 per cent of the urban population of Morocco are aware of one Christian organization's satellite TV programme and 470,000 (around 4 per cent of the population) tune in each week.[10]

- A Christian-backed musical event took place in Morocco in May 2005. Media attention caused the government to react. One American on the staff of a well-known Christian organization was subsequently refused entry to the country because of the internal disquiet over the amount of Christian activity. The media has confirmed that an unprecedented number of Moroccans are following Christ.[11]

- Amer (name changed) is from one of the nations of the Middle East that borders Israel. He moved to Egypt and graduated in Islamic Law from Al-Azhar University in Cairo. This is one of the most prestigious orthodox Sunni institutions in the Islamic world. Amer was a radical who became a violent *jihadic* activist. He ended up in Khartoum, the capital of Sudan. One evening he was praying alone in a mosque. The voice of Jesus boomed into the mosque asking, 'Why are you persecuting me?' At the same time the glass window high above Amer shattered and Qur'ans toppled off shelves onto the floor. This supernatural intervention triggered Amer's search for Jesus. He soon took the dangerous step of becoming one of his followers.

- A nationally respected Protestant minister in one Middle Eastern country told me that within a ten-year period, ministers of almost every denomination, including Orthodox priests, had begun to get involved in counselling and baptizing people from Muslim backgrounds. A friend of mine who was a team leader for twelve years with a western organization in that country told me that his team had baptized more Muslims during that year alone than in the previous eleven years.

- A conservative estimate of the numbers of Muslims following Jesus in Indonesia and Bangladesh combined runs into many hundreds of thousands. There is little or no western involvement in these movements. These new believers are setting up indigenous worshipping communities that are totally appropriate to their cultural context. A British researcher visited one group where a congregation leader reported that they had five hundred followers of Jesus waiting to be baptized in that group alone.

- Research has gone on into why and how Muslims are following Jesus. One survey used a sample of six hundred Muslim background followers of Jesus around the world that were willing to give responses to questions about how and why they were following Christ.[12]

Beware – God is at work!

God is not only touching Muslims but he is also gently creating a new climate of faith for them among

Christians. Open Doors with Brother Andrew ended a seven-year prayer initiative for the Communist world in 1989 – the year the Berlin Wall came down. They then embarked on a ten-year prayer initiative for the Muslim world. In 2000, I visited the World Prayer Centre directed by Dr C. Peter Wagner in Colorado Springs. My aim was to familiarize myself with their 'state of the art' technology, which they are using to track the millions of Christians around the world who are praying for Muslims, especially during the Ramadan month of fasting and the five day *hajj* pilgrimage when up to four million Muslims converge on Mecca. Shortly after my visit to the Centre, Peter Wagner reported that the intercessory networks for Muslims around the world were growing so fast, they had become impossible to count and were therefore humanly 'out of control'. God is initiating this prayer thrust for the remaining unreached.

What began as droplets of Muslims following Christ in the 1980s became a trickle in the 1990s and a tiny flow around the turn of the millennium. The attacks in America on 11 September 2001 proved to be another factor that compelled Christians to pray; it also loosened the heart allegiance of thousands of Muslims from their traditional structures, causing them to turn to Jesus Christ.

The flow is not yet a flood, nevertheless Christian leaders in the Muslim world tell me that the phenomenon of Muslim enquirers who want to talk through their spiritual issues is now a daily occurrence. The baptism of believers from Muslim backgrounds has also become a regular feature of local church life in several Muslim lands.

The Great Commission contains no exclusion clause for Muslims. God loves them as much as anyone else. His grace is actively seeking them out right where they are both within the Muslim world and in the West. Western Christians need to hear more about this side of the equation. This aspect is the upside that encourages us to identify with what God is doing and to consider adopting a grace-response to the Muslim. But there is also a downside – as we shall see next.

Notes

1. Patrick Johnstone, The Keswick Lecture, 2003 (available from ICC Eastbourne www.iccspreadingtheword.com).
2. Friday Fax email bulletin of world mission, June 2005.
3. Brother Andrew, 'The Greatest Challenge facing the western church today' (*Christian Herald*, 23 July 2005), p15.
4. D. Barrett, *Statistical Table on World Mission*, (Virginia Beach: Regent University, 2004).
5. Richard Spencer, 'Christianity is China's new social revolution' (*Daily Telegraph*, 30 July 2005), p14.
6. Friday Fax June (Libya) and February (Iran) 2005, *Ahl-i Kitab* June Newsletter 2005;
   Agape Voice (Indian Punjab figures) Friday Fax Alex Abraham, June 2005;
   'Sharing God's Love' in *Witness – The Voice of the Persecuted Church* magazine, Release International, Issue 26, July 2005, p3.
7. Bilquis Sheikh, *I Dared to Call Him Father* (Eastbourne: Kingsway Publications, 1978).
8. David S. Bentley, *The 99 Beautiful Names of God* (Pasadena: William Carey Library, 1999).
9. *Christian Herald*, World News, 4 June 2005, p5.
10. *Uplink* – Quarterly News, Spring 2005.
11. *Daily Telegraph*, May 2005.
12. J. Dudley Woodberry & Russell G. Shubin, *Muslims tell "Why I chose Jesus"* (Pasadena: USCWM, Mission Frontiers Magazine, March 2001), p28.

Chapter 6

Grace for Muslims?

*What is it about my faith (Islam) that turns people into
demons while they belong to a faith which, if you look at the
five pillars, is an extraordinary benign religion.*
Yasmin Alibhai-Brown
(Readers Digest, March 2006)

I was driving north on the A1 after a conference for
mission leaders when I casually turned on the radio to
catch a news bulletin on the hour. The news was already
in full flow and the anchor person was giving a report
about an accident involving a high-rise building. I
assumed it was Canary Wharf in London but I was
wrong. The tower was the World Trade Center; the place
was New York City and the date was 11 September 2001.
It was a day that changed the world.

It certainly changed my life because from then on God
started to prepare me to move on alone. Staff changes at
Action Partners made it a convenient time for them and
me to part company after my nine years as International
Director. 9/11 acted as a trigger that helped me make up
my mind to step out and make myself available full-time

to British Christians as a consultant in Islam and Christian witness. It was clear that the need in Britain was only going to increase, so by May 2002 I had left the mission and become a self-employed consultant; a role that officially started on the first anniversary of 9/11 (11 September 2002).

At last Christians started to acknowledge the presence of Muslims but for all the wrong reasons. Many Muslims were feeling vulnerable and even embarrassed by 9/11. I sensed a general concern that the Muslim and western worlds might embark on a course leading to a clash of ideologies. 9/11 not only provoked the East/West clash Osama Bin Laden had hoped for, it also sparked a clash among Muslims as they disagreed about what the essential Islamic way should be and how Islam can co-exist with the non-Muslim world.

I was encouraged by a burly Pentecostal minister in Manchester who told me how a young Pakistani couple living close to him just needed a big hug – which he obligingly gave them. At that time it was significant if a white person or a Muslim extended a hand of friendship across the divide of bewilderment. Relationship was the issue so I called my consultant service Friendship First[1] with the purpose statement, 'Opening the way for Christian witness'. The aim was to replicate myself by helping ordinary Christians to discuss the good news about Jesus with ordinary Muslims. I knew that I could only talk to one Muslim at a time but if I touched the lives of ten thousand Christians, ten thousand such conversations would become possible at the same time. So Friendship First was born and a training manual and website followed shortly afterwards.

In one church a lady asked me, 'Are the Islams the ones with the red spot on their forehead?' I could see that I had my work cut out. My answer was, 'If they are Islams, you are a Christianity, and it's Hindus not Muslims who have a red spot on their foreheads.' I had to come to terms with the fact that the average church member knew very little about Muslims and what they did know was sometimes muddled up with Hindus and Sikhs. This lack of general awareness has drastically changed over the past five years. Looking back I feel a sense of satisfaction that I have been a small part of promoting this change. I have worked hard at supplying what was lacking for British Christians. To do this I listed the needs using the five English vowel sounds.

A – attitude . . . the need for attitude change towards Muslims

E – emotion . . . the need to be free of the negative emotion of fearing Muslims

I – information . . . the need for balanced information about Muslims

O – opportunity . . . the need for a mechanism through which to meet real live Muslims

U – understanding . . . the need to understand with biblical balance and have faith for Muslims

What British Christians think

One day I was driving down a road near our home. The weather was cold and drizzling. I spotted a Pakistani lady walking along, trying to keep her head dry by holding a plastic shopping bag over it. She reminded me of the women I would see in Egypt carrying things on their heads with perfect balance. I felt for this woman whom I suspected had been lifted by circumstances right out of her eastern environment and dropped into British society. She seemed so far from home and she looked so out of place as she trudged along wearing only a cardigan over her traditional *shalwâr kames* (traditional baggy clothing). On top of her bewilderment in British society, this lady now faced the added burden of 9/11 and the further isolation this brought to her community.

As I drove past her I prayed that she would somehow have the opportunity to hear the good news about Jesus from someone in her network of relationships – whether Asian or western. I was having an instinctive – grace-response towards this Muslima (female *muslîm*). I could not get to her, yet somehow it felt possible to touch her life by praying for her.

Later in the same week I happened to be in the car park of a cinema complex in the West Midlands where I saw a middle class white couple saying goodbye to Pakistani friends. The Muslim couple had three beautiful daughters who were all dressed in quality *shalwars*. The girls clambered into the back of the family's top-of-the-range 4x4 vehicle while the mother exchanged a hug and a kiss with her white lady friend and the men shook hands warmly. It was a two-way grace-response to and from Muslims.

Shortly after this incident a minister friend of mine in Birmingham told me how his Muslim next-door-neighbour came to say goodbye on the day my friend was moving house. The Muslim stood holding my friend's hand in the street when, he broke down in tears and said, 'I have always wanted to live next door to a man of God and now you are leaving us.'

On another occasion the same minister said that this same Muslim called him 'one in the million'. He was the first committed Christian the Muslim had ever met in the UK. In Islamic terms, such a believing person may be called by the Arabic word *mu'min* (a true believer and godly person) regardless of the religious tradition they are from. Muslims do react positively to spiritual reality in the lives of western followers of Jesus, so relating to a Muslim is not a 'specialist' thing but within the grasp of every Christian.

I became convinced that even in a climate of suspicion it is possible for the draft of grace to blow both ways and that relationships can and should be developed between Christians and Muslims in the West. On issues such as the battle against aggressive secularism Christians and Muslims stand on similar ground. If only both groups would recognize that fact.

I was concerned to discover that most Christians tend to only see the negatives, which leads to an attitude problem towards Muslims. I wondered what it would take for Christians to have their eyes opened to what God is doing with and through Muslims. Should Christians ask themselves why, at a time when Europe is so secularized, God has chosen to allow over fifteen million Muslims to settle here? And what might God be saying to the marginalized western church, struggling with its spiritual mandate; or to western governments and to secular society? Christians seem happy to agree that God's ways are not our ways (Is. 55:8-9) but they are prone to panic when God behaves in ways they cannot understand or approve of.

One such Christian challenged me publicly when I appealed for prayer that God would give a Damascus Road experience to extremists such as Osama Bin Laden and his number two man Ayman Zawaheri. This Christian insisted that these men are 'instruments in the purposes of God' and should therefore be left alone. The inference was that these men are on a par with Judas Iscariot and therefore already assigned a place in hell. This logic puts some Muslims beyond the scope of prayer; a questionable position for any Christian to take.

Logic tells us that those who crucified Jesus were similarly motivated by the powers of darkness and were no less 'instruments in God's purpose', yet Jesus prayed for them from the very Cross they had put him on. So even if it could be shown that some Muslims were beyond redemption, who are we to decide who is and who is not in that category?

Thankfully, to balance this sort of negativity I began to hear some exciting anecdotes about the positive interaction of Christians with Muslims. It was as if 9/11 had caused some Christians to stop looking straight through British Muslims and start to notice them.

On one occasion when I was leading a Friendship First Muslim awareness seminar in a multi-cultural community in Lancashire – England's 'deep north' – a man said, 'Some of the best Christians in this area are Muslims.' This caused a hearty laugh. However, this wisecrack posed a disturbing question. How could some Muslims be in some way more 'Christian' than a Christian? During another Friendship First training session for church-planters a man told the group (seriously this time) how a close relative of his had been ill in a South African hospital. Her Muslim neighbours had been the ones to visit her most regularly. Apparently these Muslims could not do enough to help; they even offered to 'keep her in their prayers' in an evangelical style.

I found an article in a national newspaper reporting on a Catholic priest who collapsed and died after saving a group of small children from drowning in a lakeside incident in Italy. My initial reaction was how Christ-like this act of selflessness was. The very next day I spotted another article in another newspaper; this time it was about a thirty-six-year-old man from Bradford, West Yorkshire. He also died but this time after chasing a getaway van from a £40,000 armed robbery. The van eventually stopped and a man got out and shot the pursuing man through the heart at near point-blank range. The man's wife was four months pregnant. The public-spirited man did not live to see his baby daughter, who was called Rafia. Yes, the father-to-be was a Muslim. His name was Tasawar Hussain.

My reactions to this man were mixed. It made me feel uneasy when it dawned on me that the Muslim had acted in exactly the same selfless way as the Catholic priest at the lakeside. My problem was how to admit that a Muslim had done the 'Christ-like' thing. The action of the Catholic priest, although following Jesus in an entirely different tradition to mine, was nevertheless more accessible to me because he was in a 'Christian' category. But here was the rub. What when someone from a creed that I neither share nor accept models my own Christ-centred values from within that creed?

Jesus said, 'Greater love has no man than this, that a man lay down his life for his friends' (Jn. 15:13 RSV). When Tasawar's murderers were sentenced it transpired that the shop they had robbed was owned by a Muslim. I thought I had found grounds to go easy on myself, 'Isn't it merely a case of one Muslim looking after another?' I thought. This shamed me even more because the person Tasawar laid his life down for was a Muslim that he did not even know – let alone call 'friend'.[2]

I could not think of a reason why the 'someone' who laid down their life could not be a Muslim immigrant any more than a Samaritan could not be the hero to the man who fell among thieves in the parable (Lk. 10:30-37). The Samaritans were a longstanding immigrant people in ancient Israel. The battle with prejudice was evidently not quite won in me yet.

Combating the issues behind our prejudice

Sometimes it is a thankless task to stand between the Christian and the Muslim for the sake of Jesus Christ but I have learned to take comfort from the words of Jesus the Master reconciler who said, 'Blessed are the peacemakers for they will be called children of God' (Mt. 5:9). Although I have frequently felt like dropping the whole Muslim issue, I have been constantly renewed in this task by the love of Christ in me for the Muslim (2 Cor. 5:14). Someone once said that people need less promotion of the Gospel and more free samples; these can only come from Jesus Christ through us. At times I have felt like asking God to take his love for the Muslim away from me but it simply will not go away.

I am convinced that the Spirit of God is saying to the whole of his church that it is possible for Christian/ Muslim relationships to be marked less by doctrinal bickering and more by the gracious spirit of Jesus. When a Muslim is confronted by a western follower of Jesus who is 'in the West but not of it' they are usually intrigued. One way to be not 'of' the West is to love the Muslim. Since the inception of Friendship First on 11 September 2002, I have had to wrestle with answers to the questions posed by the Muslim presence in western societies; so far I have found eleven good reasons why it is appropriate for a Christian to extend grace towards a Muslim.

1. Grace because it's not their fault

Unlike the westerner who has the choice in life about what they want to be and do, a Muslim is born with an automatic identity and role that overlays both birth and culture. They are not brought up in Islam and then allowed to choose whether or not to continue with it into adulthood. They are 'in' Islam whether they like it or not and, as such, they are obliged to abide by Islam's social control which goes further than the state regulations of Marxism. Islam lays claim to the very soul of a Muslim in a way that atheistic Marxism never could.

The Islamic worldview is a corporate one that says 'I am because we are'.[3] From the age of puberty onwards, the community recognizes an adult and pro-actively encourages them to adhere to Islam's prescribed social duties. This is expressed in the proverb 'It takes the community to raise one child.' *The Times*[4] reported the story of how a young British-born Pakistani Muslim called Ahmer Khokhar became a follower of Jesus. The news reached his father who was a community leader; these are the power-brokers who regulate Muslim societies. The pressure was so great that Ahmer felt no option but to emigrate to Australia.

Patrick Johnstone describes this Islamic form of social control as follows.

> The close-knit Muslim community is an entrenched cultural web that enmeshes people into deep loyalty to the system. The strong underlying adherence to family and community customs, makes an individual decision for Christ almost impossible without fatally injuring these relational links. Therefore the cost of discipleship in a Muslim community is very high.[5]

So, at the level of family, community and the Islamic state, the Muslim is not offered many choices in life. This scenario is seen by some westerners as a form of 'spiritual communism' while the Muslim mind sees western society as morally bankrupt and a spiritual Babylon.

Muslims are born bonded to a well-defined system that has religious, political, moral, legal and social aspects. For centuries they have remained in an uninformed twilight zone with regard to Jesus Christ. Kenneth Cragg is right when he calls for 'the restoration to Muslims of the Christ whom they have always missed'.[6] It is not their fault.

2. *Grace because Muslims are here in the purposes of God*

If God is the sovereign Lord of history (as he is) the Muslim presence in the West must be part of his purpose. The Apostle Paul said, 'God determined the exact places where humankind should live . . . so they may reach out for him and find him' (Acts 17:26-27 NIV).

Dr Peter Cotterell, a past principal of the London School of Theology, worked as a Christian mission partner in Africa for many years. When he came back to live in south London he felt irritated that 'they' (i.e. Asian immigrants) had 'taken over my town'. One morning he was reading his Bible when he came across the words 'The earth is the Lord's and everything in it, the world and all who live in it . . . ' (Ps. 24:1). This challenged Peter about whose community it was – God's or his. He took the point and has lived in the light of its implications ever since.

I believe the Muslim presence may actually be the will of God because the movement of peoples was common in Old Testament times where the influences of alien cultures such as Assyria and Babylonia were used by God to correct ancient Israel's departure from his ways. It is not hard to see a parallel today. Whether this analysis is correct or not, God has allowed the influx of God-fearing Muslims at precisely the time when European societies are walking away from the Judeo-Christian principles, in favour of godless secularism. Muslims are among us for a reason.

3. Grace because Islam is incompatible with the post-modern world

I was browsing in the departure lounge of Sydney International Airport, when I was struck by a bookcase containing no less than nine separate paperbacks featuring the harrowing stories of Muslim women in various parts of the world from Sudan to Afghanistan.

Take, for example, Saudi Arabian TV presenter Rania al-Baz, whose face was beaten to a pulp by her angry husband. It was likely that no more would have been done about this had Rania not been willing to invite her media contacts to come to her hospital bedside. They took 'before' and 'after' photographs of her face, which were sent around the world. This forced the Saudi police to put out a warrant for the husband's arrest.[7]

Amina Lawal is a young northern Nigerian woman who had an illegitimate baby. She was charged with adultery and sentenced to death by stoning in a *shari'a* court. This case sparked an international protest that forced the court to quash the conviction and grant a pardon.[8] Western Christians still ask me the loaded question, 'Where do Muslims get this sort of barbaric behaviour from?' The simple answer is, straight out of the Jewish Torah.

Iranian lay-pastor Hamid Pourmand began following Christ over twenty years ago while serving in the army. Documentary proof exists that his superiors knew of his conversion yet they promoted him to the rank of Colonel. All was well until his sudden arrest on 9 September 2004. He was held in solitary confinement until 13 April 2005 when he was formally charged with apostasy and proselytizing Muslims. When he refused to return to Islam he was sentenced to death. His appeal against the decision attracted media attention, which led to Hamid's sudden acquittal. As the judge dropped the charges his reported words were, 'I don't know who you are but the rest of the world does'.[9]

Some aspects of *shari'a* law and some pre-Islamic cultural practices are incompatible with the UN International Charter of Human Rights; for example, female circumcision; honour killing; Shi'ite child flagellation; the persecution of Muslims who leave the faith; the physical abuse of children in mosques; multiple marriages and the male subjugation of women.[10] Such issues are being challenged by human rights groups, the media and politicians.

Researcher Bernard Lewis referred to the 'historical incompatibility of Islam and democracy'. He outlined how, in Christendom's history, there has been a tradition of councils, synods and assemblies that were the precursor to the concept of parliament and representational democracy. Lewis concludes that

> Almost all aspects of Muslim government have an intensely personal character. In principle, at least, there is no state, but only a ruler; no court, but only a judge. There is not even a city with defined powers, limits and functions, but only an assemblage of neighbourhoods, mostly defined by family, tribal, ethnic or religious criteria, and governed by officials, usually military, appointed by the sovereign. The legislative power of a western democratic parliament is out of step with the tenor of Islam, in that Islam is in principle a theocracy – a state ruled by God through revelation. Disobedience is a sin as well as a crime.[11]

In 2003 eighty Islamic nations came to together in Kuala Lumpur, Malaysia, to consider the future of Islam in a globalized world. Muslims are becoming increasingly aware that they have to come to terms with life in the non-Muslim world which is co-dependent with the West for survival. The Iranian journalist, Amir Taheri, when assessing the Kuala Lumpur conference, urged Muslims to end the 'culture of blame' and face the challenge of arguing Islam's case against western secularism in the 'marketplace of ideas' rather than allowing the lunatic fringe to resort to flying planes into buildings, which he said was 'a poor substitute for logical debate'. He continued

> The theo-political discourse that is designed to limit free-dom of thought and expression in the Muslim world is a relatively new phenomenon developed by a small number of militant Islamic thinkers influenced by Western totali-tarian ideologies, especially communism and fascism.
>
> It is therefore perfectly possible for Muslims to develop modern and democratic societies in the era of globalization. But to do that they have to understand that religion is part of life, not the other way round as the theo-political discourse suggests.[12]

Islam is facing pressure to undergo some sort of reform. The same influence that has been brought to bear on the behaviour of some American troops in Iraq's Abu Ghraib prison and Guantanamo Bay is also being applied to the behaviour of radical Muslims.

4. *Grace because, like the church, Islam is a house divided*

Internal friction has been a theme in Islamic history ever since the birth of Ishmael. God said he would live 'at odds' with all his brothers (Gen. 16:12b) and his descendants have been doing so ever since. There is an Arab proverb that says, 'I against my brother; I and my brother against our cousin; I and my brother and our cousin against the world.' I find this to be a revealing insight into the Arab mindset in particular and Muslim societies in general.

Although Christianity is about the grace of God in Christ, from the birth of the church, Christians have had a legacy of theological in-fighting punctuated by occasional physical fighting; some people would include the Northern Ireland troubles as a case in point. In the House of Islam it has almost been the reverse; throughout Islam's history there has been armed conflict going on somewhere in the Muslim world punctuated by occasional periods of theological in-fighting. For example, since the second Gulf War two Saudi groups, the Wahabi and the Selaffi, have joined forces with Al-Qaeda to fight the newly installed Iraqi government. At the same time, in the heartland of Saudi Arabia, Al-Qaeda and the ruling class are enemies. Al-Qaeda have bombed Saudi interests to punish the royal household of *Sa'ud* for being too pro-American.

Then there is the Sunni/Shi'a division which works in a similar way to the Catholic/Protestant divide. The core issue here is the different understanding about the apostolic succession to the leadership (*Caliphate*) after the death of Muhammad. Today 80 per cent of Muslims are Sunni, 10 per cent are Shi'a and the rest are a variety of smaller groupings including the Suffi and the Ahmadiyya. There has been a long-standing Sunni/Shi'a tension in the border regions of Pakistan and Afghanistan, but more notably in Iraq, which was a traditionally Shi'a nation until the Shi'a community was suppressed for thirty years by the Sunni minority under Saddam Hussein.

I have seen Muslims shooting at each other from rival mosques on opposite sides of the same street in the north-west frontier of Pakistan. The police have had to be called to British mosques on a number of occasions where fist fights have broken out among rival factions. In Luxor, Egypt, I saw a line of men united in the evening prayers only to finish, roll their prayer mats up and continue a mass brawl that had evidently started just before the call to prayer. They had simply paused for prayer before resuming hostilities.

Moderate and militant Muslims are becoming polarized in a battle to achieve *muhâsaba* (agreement) about an authentic Islamic voice and when military *jihad* is legitimate. Amir ul-Haq, a PhD student at Goldsmiths College London found that the 'electrical charge' of religion is changing the disenchantment of young Muslims into something far more dangerous. These youngsters feel they are Muslim first and British second. The role models for this thinking were more likely to be ex-*mujahideen* who had survived in Bosnia and Afghanistan. 'These are the voices that are influencing the younger generation, not the establishment voices of reason.'[13]

Which Islam will prevail in the twenty-first century – orthodox Islam, liberal Islam, fundamentalist Islam, militant Islam or a new spiritual Islam? Islam is a house divided (Mk. 3:25).

5. *Grace because Muslims are harassed by the powers of darkness*

During my early weeks in Egypt I was woken up by the *muezzin's* call to prayer at three-thirty in the morning. The room was filled with a dark and menacing presence. Rather than jumping to the conclusion that Muslims or their culture were intrinsically evil, it had the opposite effect on me. I felt even more bonded to the local people because their worldview exposed them to harrassment in this way by the spirit world.

Many Muslims look for spiritual protection from wherever they can get it. Some consult magical practitioners, which are often women who have been on the *hajj* and who have a 'gift' in the magic art of negotiating with the powers of darkness. It is also fairly common for Muslims to ask Christian ministers to pray for them in the name of Jesus, the recognized healing prophet in the Qur'an.

Bill Musk discusses this area more fully in his book *The Unseen Face of Islam*.[14] He also comments as follows.

> There can be considerable concern among our Muslim neighbours about the activities of spirits, the bane of demon possession, the power of curses and the need for protection from unseen – but hostile – beings and forces. Questions are consequently raised for Christians, especially Western-educated ones, about the realness of the world that such Muslims seem to live in.
>
> Fortunately there are some helpful hints, for Christians . . . in their own Bible. Western Christians need to become interpreters of the (unseen spirit realm) . . . from a biblical perspective for their Muslim friends. It is no coincidence that many of the most successful missions have provided some form of Christian answer to (spirit world) questions.[15]

6. Grace because Muslims are supportive of Judeo-Christian moral values

American-born billionaire Jean Paul Getty[16] was said to be the richest man in the world. He lived in England for many years before he died in 1976 aged eighty-four.

Although Getty subscribed to no religious faith, his business acumen gave him remarkable insight into world affairs. As early as 1975 he saw the potential 'demise' of western civilization. Although he knew Muslims in political high places in the Middle East, he was sure that the western demise would come, not from an external source, such as Islam, but from a less obvious source – liberalism. He did not fear Muslims but he did fear the moral decline in the West.

Thirty years after his prediction, many people would agree with Getty that there has been an over-liberalizing of western culture in general and European culture in particular. For example, twelve-year-old children are now receiving nicotine patches from school nurses to help them break their addiction to smoking.[17] Other features of British society include binge-drinking, the highest teenage pregnancy rate in Europe, crimes of violence, over-crowded prisons, criminals being treated more like victims, marital breakdowns, social unrest, anti-social teenagers, bullying in schools and pupil aggression against teachers. A battle is raging within traditional denominations over the permitted sexual orientation of their ministers. The sub-text to this battle is the issue of the authority of the Bible across time and cultures.

A Christian doctor, who campaigns against medically assisted suicide, asked me in preparation for a radio interview, if it would be true to say that Muslims agreed with Christians on these issues. Of course the answer was 'yes' and would be on most ethical issues. When Mary Whitehouse, the campaigner for moral standards in the media and in public life, died, Dr Majid Katme of *Islamic Concern* in London, wrote to a Christian newspaper to say

As a Muslim, I was, over the years, inspired and moved by her holy campaign (i.e. jihadic action) to protect our children and all of society; to us Muslims, her campaign is an Islamic campaign and it is our duty as Muslim believers to join her and support her. I wanted so much to say to Mary before she died: Thank you for what you have done. Thank you for alerting us Muslims to this great danger; thank you for giving us hope.[18]

Muslims burnt their TV licences, alongside Christians, outside BBC Broadcasting House London in protest against the TV screening of *Jerry Springer – the Opera* in January 2005. During the question time, following a talk I gave at a conference for evangelical Anglican clergy and spouses, one minister told me how Muslim leaders in Wolverhampton had challenged a ministers' fraternal for not speaking up enough for Jesus Christ.

If Jean Paul Getty was alive today, he would not excuse the politically motivated fanaticism of some Muslims. Neither would he see the Muslim presence in the West as the threat that many Christians think it is. In an age of moral demise, Getty would not see Muslims as the cause of such demise, but a steadying influence during it.

I believe that the presence of Muslims in the West should be seen by Christians as a kind of spiritual reinforcement in the battle for biblical morality in a society where secularism is its biggest threat.

7. *Grace because of Islam's elder brother sensitivities*

Although Islam appears to be powerful in terms of its ability to mount violent demonstrations at short notice, nevertheless it is insecure. I call this phenomenon the 'elder brother syndrome'. I coined this expression to account for the animosity which runs between Christian and Muslim both ways, because both feel threatened by the other. Both assume that they are the senior party:

Christianity on the grounds that Christ is the Omega, the final revelation of God with a six-hundred years start over Islam. Islam, however, sees the same six-hundred years time lapse as evidence of its youth and therefore a chronological advantage over Christianity. Islam claims to have gathered up the best of both Judaism and Christianity into itself, making both of its older cousins redundant.

By 'elder brother syndrome' I am referring to the attitude and actions of a first-born who becomes defensive and protective – even violent – in order to safeguard their position against a perceived threat from competing siblings. It is a form of sibling rivalry.

Judaism reacted negatively to the birth of Christianity, calling it a heretical sect. Later on, the Christian church had a similar reaction to the birth of Islam, which some referred to as 'Mohammadanism'. In its turn, Islam developed a similar attitude to both Judaism and Christianity. Over the centuries Christianity and Islam have moved from being 'kissing cousins' to 'bickering cousins' and even 'kicking cousins'. The roots of the problem go back to the original tension over the status of Ishmael as Abraham's first-born in Genesis 16. Ishmael personified the self-help or 'works' ethos while Isaac personified the divine assistance of grace.[19] The resulting friction was played out against the background of dysfunctional family relationships.

Ishmael's birth provoked competitiveness between him and Isaac (Gal. 4:23a). This was particularly the case because Isaac's apparently unfair advantage over his elder brother came about by a 'divine promise' (Gal. 4:23b). Ishmael resented the fact that Isaac received something he did not have to work for. Another point of friction was that Isaac's line became the custodians of the 'everlasting covenant' (Gen. 17:19). This denied Ishmael his culturally recognized birthright. These boys were born into, and symbolically lived out, the 'works/grace' tension. God would become known as the 'God of Abraham, Isaac and Jacob' – but never Ishmael. It went against the culture to say this, as it inflicted a stigma on Ishmael. This compounded the marginalization that Ishmael felt after his rejection by Sarah and Abraham. The apparent injustice was on a par with God saying – 'Jacob have I loved and Esau have I hated' (Mal. 1:2, 3; Rom. 9:13).

The elder brother syndrome is a recurring theme through the Bible:

- Cain and Abel (Gen. 4:1-9)

  Cain worked hard on the land and was jealous of God's favour on Abel the herdsman.
- Ishmael and Isaac (Gen. 21:8-10)

  Ishmael reacted to the favour poured on Isaac by Sarah and Abraham. Likewise, the descendants of Ishmael and Isaac experienced tension and insisted on no intermarriage (Gen. 28:6-9).
- Esau and Jacob (Gen. 25:27-34; Gen. 27)

  Jacob, the younger son, stole the elder brother's birthright and thereby inherited Esau's blessing.
- Perez and Zerah (Gen. 38:27-30)

  Like Jacob, Perez got ahead of his elder brother and received preferential treatment.
- Benjamin the youngest (Gen. 43:32-34)

  Joseph broke the cultural norm of favouring the eldest by making a point of heaping favour on Benjamin the youngest.
- Manasseh and Ephraim (Gen. 48:12-20)

  Jacob perpetuated the 'elder shall serve the younger' pattern twice, once when he favoured Joseph and secondly when he crossed his hands over to bless

Ephraim the younger son instead of Manasseh the elder.

The syndrome was described by Jesus in the parable of the Prodigal Son. To the minds of Jesus' Middle Eastern audience, the story is shocking because it is the elder brother who acted in the culturally *appropriate* way, both by his loyalty to the father while the prodigal was gone and also by his anger when he returned. The elder brother's words revealed his 'performance based' mentality.

> 'All these years I have been *slaving* for you and *never disobeyed* your orders. Yet *you never* even gave me a young goat so I could celebrate with my friends. But when this son of yours who has squandered your property with prostitutes comes home, you kill the fatted calf for him.' (Lk. 15:29-30).

The elder brother worked for his share of the father's inheritance (Lk. 15:25a, 29). He was angry and frustrated by the apparent injustice of grace (Lk. 15:29b-30). On the other hand, it was the younger brother's childlike trust in the father's grace that was judged by Jesus to be so acceptable in the Kingdom. 'I will go back to my father and say I have sinned . . . please take me' (Lk. 15:18-19). Jesus almost woos his audience into supporting the reaction of the elder brother who refused to join in the father's celebration (Lk. 15:28a).

This celebration for the younger brother is paralleled by Abraham's feast to celebrate Isaac's long-awaited arrival (Gen. 21:8). The punchline would make the air crackle with the outrageous fact that self-help was made inferior to grace. This would be a bitter pill to swallow for anyone coming from a performance-based religion, such as

Judaism or Islam. Grace is the core of the Gospel which is a key reason for the negative reaction of many Muslims to it.

I notice that the Apostle Paul alluded to the elder brother syndrome when he pointed to its expression through violence; 'the son born in the ordinary way persecuted the son born by the power of the Spirit. It is the same now' (Gal. 4:29). This insight helped me see why it might be that Jewish extremists should attack the early church and also why, in the 1960s and 1970s, the emerging Messianic groups were opposed by the modern state of Israel. Statistically speaking, Christians are the biggest casualty of persecution in Muslim lands today. This is not to say that fundamentalist Jews and Muslims are consciously reacting to grace, but what I am suggesting is that, like Saul of Tarsus who 'kicked against the goads' of grace (Acts 26:14), there may also be some principle at work in the Muslim reaction to the Gospel.

I believe the elder brother syndrome lies behind the inability of many Muslims to admit when arguing with non-Muslim westerners that, on some points, they may be wrong. Peter Riddell sees a pattern whereby Muslims 'close ranks in times of difficulty, rather than engage in necessary self-criticism'. Professor Riddell cites a notable Muslim journalist Ziauddin Sardar who said, 'Muslims are quick to note the double-standards of America, but we seldom question our own double-standards.'[20]

I often need grace in order not to become irritated when I try to reason with an unreasonable Muslim. But even with these Muslims, it is when we are able to stand just a little closer to where they stand that we begin to appreciate Bill Musk's words: 'The most helpful insights often emerge when people of different faiths become attuned to each other's wavelengths of thought and manage to feel their way into the other's heart.'[21]

8. *Grace because radical Islam may be passing its zenith*

In July 2005 King Abdullah of Jordan hosted a conference. One hundred and seventy Islamic scholars and
intellectuals were there from both Sunni and Shi'a
traditions. The participants represented all eight schools
of Islamic law, which made their conclusions significant.
In a written statement, these leading clerics from all over
the Muslim world denounced the doctrine of *takfir*
(declaration of enemy-Muslims as infidels) as currently
used by extremists; they also denounced any 'perverse
and unqualified misuse of *fatwas*'. This signalled the
intention to reaffirm their traditional spiritual authority
in the Muslim *umma.* They see this authority as being
usurped by extremist elements.[22]

The household of Islam is struggling internally with
conflicting views about how Islam should be practised in
the twenty-first century. Islam will not disappear but
there is evidence that a reforming process is going on. I
have already alluded to the pressure of international
human rights and the divisiveness of extremist groups
such as Al-Qaeda but we can add to these the effects of
globalization on Islam, as young Muslims everywhere
are exposed to other worldviews via the internet.
American analyst Theodore Dalrymple sees the
'shrillness' of extreme Islamic rhetoric as 'the withdrawing roar' in which 'fanatics and bombers do not
represent a resurgence of unreformed Islam but its death
rattle'.[23]

Journalist Fouad Ajami claims there is a 'battle under
way for the soul of Islam', which pits 'mainstream
modernists against cruel bigots with a warped version of
the faith'. Ajami takes the Canadian dissident Muslim
journalist Irshad Manji seriously enough to cite her
comment:

Through our screaming self-pity and our conspicuous silences, we Muslims are conspiring against ourselves. We're in crisis and we are dragging the rest of the world with us. If ever there was a moment for an Islamic reformation, it's now.[24]

Time magazine's Bill Powell quoted interviews with radical Muslims who live by the motto, 'Be proud be loud.' Powell managed to get Sheikh Khaled el-Guindi, a moderate imam from Cairo, to go on record saying,

We are passing through the hardest moments of spreading the moderate voice of our religion. These days it is extremely depressing to be a Muslim preacher with a moderate message. The surrounding circumstances form a huge stumbling block.[25]

I discovered that researchers Riddell and Cotterell identified the most urgent task facing moderate Muslims as that of discerning the principles behind Muhammad's responses to seventh-century situations that could lead away from Islam's modern propensity for conflict, based on a literal understanding of the Qur'an. They note too that Christians have had to do this for years, with the difficult biblical war texts such as those found in the book of Joshua.[26]

Analyst Ron George asserted that it is the Islamic system itself that is incapable of allowing any adjustment in order to adapt to the modern world. Furthermore 'it could not permit any blame to fall within its ranks'. For George, the attack on the World Trade Center was a 'manifestation of male frustration which was unable to see Islam itself as the root cause of the social problems of the Muslim world, and an attempt to transfer the blame onto the West.' He continues,

Islam has not delivered the goods that the West has, such as freedom of expression, advances in technology, medical knowledge, space exploration, culture and education. Islam is therefore fighting for its own life. The youth of Islamic lands is accessing data, information, styles, music, ideas, pictures and attitudes from the internet and satellite TV. This in turn makes them question the ability of Islam to deliver the same goods, to ask questions no cleric has the answer for, and to look to the West as the information provider.[27]

Muslim spokesman Shahad Aman Allah commented that 'Salman Rushdie, even if seen as an outsider to the Muslim fold, has nonetheless prompted the question of the need for Islamic institutions to rethink Islam in the twenty-first century in ways that are consonant with Islamic values and the modern world.'[28]

9. *Grace because Islam may claim more ideals than secularism*

Muslims have a higher regard for the Judeo-Christian moral framework than most secular westerners. It does not help matters, therefore, when western leaders such as President George W. Bush use phrases such as 'We, the civilized world . . .' America is seen by Muslims as a world capital of guns, gays and abortions. Likewise, Prime Minister Tony Blair said, 'Unlike the Taliban, Britain knows the difference between right and wrong.' The British journalist Tom Utley responded to this as follows.

If Britain knows the difference between right and wrong – why are English football fans seen around the world as drunken hooligans? Why are we aborting 2,500 babies every week, according to National Health Service statistics? Why does Britain have the highest teenage pregnancy rate in

Europe? Why do we have the highest prison population in the western world? And why are most of our popular TV quiz shows dedicated to greed?[29]

A grace response to the Muslim means holding the West's questionable moral high-ground more lightly and approaching the Muslim sense of morality with more humility. But before we concede too much of that ground to Islamic cultures, it is important to remind ourselves of the negative side of some Muslim countries including the persecution of Muslim dissenters; the socially approved practice of son-swapping for the sexual gratification of wealthy men; and the use of 24-hour marriage certificates to facilitate the sexual needs of men while away from home. There is little moral high ground to be had in either Islamic or western cultures.

In an interview on BBC's Breakfast TV, a leading defence expert from King's College London was asked, 'Why do the younger generation of British Muslims despise British society?' His frank response startled me. It was, 'They despise British society because we have so few moral and spiritual values left.'

If only western young people were as passionate about something. Unfortunately these idealistic young Muslims overlook the fact that Muslim societies also struggle to live up to their own ideals. This battle of confused ideologies was spotted by the Archbishop of Canterbury, Dr Rowan Williams, who said:

Terrorists can have serious moral goals. While terrorism must always be condemned, it is wrong to assume its perpetrators are devoid of political rationality. It is possible to use unspeakably wicked means to pursue an aim that is shared by those who would not dream of acting in the same way; an aim that is intelligible or even desirable i.e. reverence for

God and the practice of family values as a pale reflection of the kingdom of God on earth. If we ignore this, in our criticism of Al-Qaeda, we (too) will lose the power of self-criticism and become trapped (like them) in a self-referential morality.[30]

10. *Grace because Muslims are less of a threat and more of an opportunity*

We saw earlier that God moves peoples around the planet in his sovereign purposes. This has brought Muslims into the 'free' world where they can hear the Gospel, in some ways, more easily than in the Muslim world. We saw too how Muslims share the Judeo-Christian approach to family values, which helps support clear moral values in a climate of moral convenience. These issues suggest that the presence of Muslims in the West is not all negative.

The presence of Muslims among us also provides opportunities to discuss the good news about Jesus with indigenous westerners, as people of no faith are more prepared to reclassify issues of faith as something that is pertinent in the public domain. This is no longer because of the centrality of Christianity in western culture but because of the questions raised by Islam in the West.[31]

Muslims and other faith groups make it easier for Christians to be included as a recognized 'faith community'. Christian police officers in the south of England were refused the right to be recognized as a valid society and were denied somewhere to meet in the regional police headquarters. When Muslim officers made an approach to have a place to pray, a designated religious meeting room was allocated for all faith groups. While faith groups need to preserve their distinctives, they are also going to need each other more.

What is clear is that Muslims are turning to Christ in the West; particularly asylum seekers and other vulnerable people. Many of these are coming into the orbit of caring Christians. The presence of Muslims is providing opportunities.

11. *Grace because if others can do it, so can you*

My friend John Mosey suffered at the hands of Muslims in a far more direct way than I ever have. He and his wife Lisa lost their twenty-one-year-old daughter Helga in the 1988 terrorist attack on the PanAm flight which was blown out of the sky over Lockerbie. Since the nightmare, John has found a way for his grievance to be turned into grace. In a radio interview John was asked, 'How can you forgive animals like that?' His response was pure grace. He said, 'I am a Christian and that means every wrong thing I have ever done has been forgiven by God. If he can forgive the wrong that I have done, then I must forgive others.'[32]

John tells me that he and his wife are set to 'bless Libya' by starting a charitable trust that will help meet the development needs of the country. If a grace response is possible for people who have suffered as much as John and Lisa, then it is surely possible for all of us.

What are we prepared to do about it?

I can understand the gracelessness of so many Middle Eastern situations I came across. Muslims have no specific command from Muhammad to love those outside the *umma* of Islam. Having settled back into the West, I have struggled far more with the 'un-grace' of some western Christians. Christians have a specific command from Christ to communicate the good news about him but more disturbingly this is to be carried out under the constraint of love (2 Cor. 5:14). Every Christian has an obligation to see all types and conditions of people as coming within the scope of the love of God in Christ; and as such they have the human right to hear the Gospel. I find the attitude of many Christians can be identified on a spectrum from blissfully ignorant; to disinterested; to politely critical; to judgemental; to antagonistic; to damning; to outright paranoia. Where are you? If I can create an alternative category so can anyone.

The agenda in the British church is slowly moving on from the question, 'How can the good news about Jesus be shared with people from Muslim backgrounds?' to, 'How can these people be nurtured and supported in their journey with Christ – the second most prominent prophet of Islam?' The numbers of those from Muslim backgrounds who are enquiring about Jesus in the UK looks set to grow and with it the question of how are Jesus' western followers going to respond to the eastern followers who want to join them? This is where we turn to next.

Notes

1. Friendship First is a resource service. Contact details are at the back of the book.
2. *Daily Telegraph*, 3 March 2004.
3. Bill A. Musk, *Touching the Soul of Islam* (Crowborough: MARC, 1995), p45.
4. *The Times*, 8 January 2003.
5. Patrick Johnstone, anecdotal comment used with permission.
6. Kenneth Cragg, *The Call of the Minaret* (London: Collins Flame Classics, 1986), p245-246.
7. *Daily Telegraph*, 2 May 2005.

8. *Daily Telegraph*, August 2002.

9. Barnabas Fund and Compass Direct.

10. As well as anecdotal evidence of child abuse given to me by an inner city Anglican minister, *Daily Telegraph* article, 'Elders beat children at mosques' reported on an investigation which was launched at two mosques in the East Midlands – story by Nick Britten on 12 November 2004. Also the story, 'Morality teacher at mosque jailed for beating boy' told of Muhammad Abdullah, who was sentenced to four months at Peterborough Magistrates Court for aggravated assault on an eleven-year-old-boy – story by David Sapsted on 13 October, 2004.

11. Bernard Lewis, Islam and Liberal Democracy, (*The Atlantic Monthly*, February, 1993.

12. Amir Taheri, *New York Post*.

13. Amir ul-Haq, reported by Edward Stourton in *Analysis*, 'Jihad – faithful to or subversive of the Qur'an' (BBC Radio 4, 21 July 2005).

14. Bill A. Musk, *The Unseen Face of Islam* (Oxford: Monarch, 1989).

15. Bill A. Musk, 'Serving Muslims' (*Faith to Faith Newsletter*, November 2003), p1.

16. J. Paul Getty, *As I see it – an autobiography of J. Paul Getty*, rev ed. (Los Angeles: Jean Paul Getty Trust 2003).

17. P. Stokes (*Daily Telegraph*, 21 December 2005).

18. Letter (*Christian Herald*, 18 May, 2002).

19. The works/grace tension is taught by the Apostle Paul in Galatians 4:21-31. The parallels between Judaism and Islam and those who are 'born from above' (Jn. 1:12-13) are clear.

20. Peter Riddell, 'Terrorism – Asking questions, seeking answers' (CIS Occasional Paper Series No.3, London School of Theology, January 2002).

21. Bill A. Musk, *Kissing Cousins – Christians and Muslims Face to Face* (Oxford: Monarch Books, 2005), p33.

22. S. Abdallah Schleifer, 'The Amman Initiative' (*Islamica*, Issue 14, 2005), p23-24.

23. Theodore Dalrymple, 'When Islam Breaks Down' (City Journal, Spring 2004), www.city-journal.org.

24. Fouad Ajami, citing Irshad Manji's book *The Trouble with Islam* in, *The War Within Islam* (Readers Digest, January 2005), p74-78.
25. Bill Powell, 'The Struggle within Islam' (*Time*, 20 September 2004).
26. P. Riddell and P. Cotterell, *Islam in Conflict* (Leicester: IVP, 2003), cited in an article by Mark Greene, 'Connecting with Culture' (*Christianity*, July 2005).
27. Ron George, 'The coming implosion of Islam', (*Prophecy Today*, January/February 2002), p6-9.
28. Shahad Aman Allah speaking in an interview for CNN TV News, 12 August 2005.
29. Tom Utley (*Daily Telegraph*, September 2001).
30. Reported in an article in *Daily Telegraph*, 2004.
31. Tony Payne, *Islam in our Backyard – a novel argument* (Sydney: Matthias Media, 2002), p15.
32. Reported in, 'Impossible Forgiveness' (*Idea* Jan/Feb 2005), p6, www.audiopot.org.

Chapter 7

Welcome home

'If you want to buy a stretch limo,
check the size of your garage first.'[1]

There are clearly things to consider if we want to develop
grace relationships with a Muslim, let alone if we
welcome them into the network of our local church
family. So how do we go about this? Here are some key
issues to think through.

1. Establishing grace relationships

Encounters with Muslims are an everyday thing for
many of us. To turn a routine encounter into a purposeful
one we must be intentional about it. Jesus said he would
make his followers 'fish for people' (Mt. 4:19). This
indicates a conscious effort or a purposeful activity to
develop a relationship, which takes time and patience.
When I say 'relationship' I do not mean friendship as in
so-called 'friendship evangelism'. Relational witness is
subtly different from friendship evangelism in that it is

effective in achieving the intended goal of sharing the good news about Jesus but with the added bonus that it helps us to avoid certain problems.

The first potential problem with friendship is that it becomes a loaded term when expressed from one culture to another. For instance, Muslims from some countries only enter friendship when the other person is likely to be useful to them, while other Muslims feel it is only appropriate to permit an outsider onto the periphery of their community until they prove themselves. Still other Muslims pull the outsider straight into the centre, assuming that the friend is willing to participate in a 'What's yours is mine' system. An African I knew just helped himself to the belongings of the people around him because he considered them his 'friends'. A North African tried this on me when he needed an item of clothing that he knew I had two of; at least he asked me first. The issue is what a westerner and a Muslim understand by the word 'friendship'.

Jesus defined his friends as those who 'do what I ask'. They are those who make it their business to 'know his business' and they are prepared to lay down their life for him (Jn. 15:14-15). So if by 'friend' we mean this level of commitment then it is a high ideal indeed; many Christians do not have this in mind when they think of friendship.

Secondly, the idea of 'friendship evangelism' carries with it an ethical dilemma. It is harder to maintain integrity if a friendship is merely the mechanism for evangelism. However, relational witness enables us to facilitate the faith journey of the other person while avoiding the possibility of becoming a spiritual predator. Perceptive Muslims may have a point when they react to what they see as the deceptive behaviour of Christian missionaries. We must ask ourselves whether such an approach is genuine friendship at all.

What I am calling 'relational witness' is actually 'spiritual friendship'; something that is introduced and expanded on by American author Brian D. McLaren.[2] You may feel that the distinction I am making between friendship evangelism and relational witness is only playing with words but I do not think so. I am not rejecting friendship evangelism *per se* but I am doing three things:

1. I am pointing out that Muslims and Christians sometimes mean different things when using the same word e.g. 'friendship.' Christians can also mean different things when they use the expression 'friendship evangelism' and one definition of it is more worthy than the other.
2. I am hopefully giving 'friendship evangelism' a clearer definition by focusing on the formation of a connection with a Muslim which is genuine and which fosters mutual trust, with no strings attached.
3. I am trying to show that what is widely understood as 'friendship evangelism' is not really evangelism at all but simply the means of developing a healthy context for evangelism.

I find 'relational witness' to be a more helpful term. If this is what you understand by the term 'friendship evangelism' anyway, that is all well and good. However, many Christians have not had the occasion to think this issue through and so assume that friendship should be used as a means of evangelism.

Grace relationships

I mentioned earlier in the book the advice of a Muslim who said to me, 'If you open a door, the draught blows both ways.' This is particularly true in a grace relationship, where the issue must not only be what I have to offer the other person but what I might gain in return – particularly from a Muslim. This is more humble and helps us not to miss being enriched by the other person. As we assist a Muslim to learn the way of Christ 'more adequately' (Acts 18:26), we will almost invariably gain insights into our own faith through them. In relational witness the outcome of the interaction is going to be genuinely open and free as each person

> accepts the other, not by ignoring the distance between us, but by measuring that distance accurately and by recognizing that whoever wants to cross over has the right and the freedom to do so. Only love can create the necessary conditions for the truth to emerge.[3]

We need to be secure enough to relate to a Muslim with grace, knowing that in that context 'truth' (i.e. particles of which are also buried in Islam) can emerge. Relational witness therefore requires of us and helps us to be confident enough to listen to and weigh whatever the Muslim has to offer in return, that may be of significance.

Jesus modelled the relational approach when he was faced with a young man from a lifestyle and mindset that was different to his own and 'loved him' (Mk. 10:21). Jesus' heart engaged with the young man; a sign that the draught was indeed 'blowing both ways' through the open door. The relationship was not just warm and fuzzy but was under-girded with honesty. The outcome was the opposite of what we might expect; the young man was just as free to walk away, which he did. However, he went away 'sad' not angry (Mk. 10:22), which suggests there was some connection: the relationship appeared strained rather than broken.

Relational witness aims to be honest while avoiding the danger of becoming sentimental at one extreme or manipulative at the other; a relationship that provides the context for Christian witness rather than merely being a tool to achieve it. In this way grace becomes the means, the method and the message all at the same time. The 'affection of Jesus Christ' (Phil. 1:8) is what stimulates us in such a grace response.

Grace relationships do not mean that I love Muslims *so that they will* follow Jesus; it means I want Muslims to follow Jesus *because I love them*. Grace must remain grace, irrespective of the outcome of a relationship. I have come to believe that the grace-response is the most authentically Christ-like way to relate to anyone. It is Christ, given to the other person, gift-wrapped in ordinary people like us.

2. Understand culture

To build relationship across cultures, we must understand something about culture. I was shocked when one Christian leader said to me, 'Britain doesn't have a culture; we're normal. Culture is something that foreigners bring in.' A mission leader gave a seminar to a class of Bible college students on the topic of 'the curse of culture' arguing that culture is a negative thing because it 'presents an obstacle to the communication of the Gospel'. His assumption was that the Gospel should be taken to 'heathen' cultures where it will iron out what is wrong and bring the people into 'godly ways' – i.e. the way we see and do things. Both these men are monocultural and are in danger of spiritual imperialism; exporting our own cultural patterns along with the Gospel and requiring the recipient to adopt both, thus becoming an extension of us.

This approach leads to both short-term and long-term problems. Church growth in Japan has been very slow to this day. This is thought to have resulted from the imposition of western patterns at the start of Christian mission in that country. Christianity has always been perceived as foreign and this has restricted the Gospel and it has failed to become embedded in Japanese culture. One Korean pastor said to the leaders of a western mission agency, 'Next time you plant the Gospel in an Asian society, please remember to take the plant out of its western plant pot.'

In my travels in seventy-nine countries I have found that people in each culture think their way of doing things is normal and the Christians think their way of worship is closest to the Bible. We have much to learn about the diversity that God has built into his world. In reality culture is neutral; it is the inevitable outcome of different peoples living in different environments. This is why there are so many regional variations of culture, even within the same country. Life in Britain is significantly different for the people of inner-city Manchester and the Isle of Orkney. Cultures are distinct and yet changing as new cultural imports constantly arrive; we have included everything from potatoes to cigarettes and Indian curry houses to French bistros.

Culture can be defined as a design for living; a plan by which 'society adapts itself to its physical and social environment'.[4] Culture is an expression of God's creative diversity expressing itself through humankind who God made in his own image. As such, although tainted by sin (as everything else in the creation is) culture must always have been an integral part of God's creation-order; it should therefore come under the category of being essentially 'very good' (Gen. 1:31).

In the Bible the language component of culture was judged at the Tower of Babel. However, this was not

because language is evil but because it had become a
vehicle of an arrogant defiance of God (Gen. 11:1-9). The
Bible simply notes that culture exists in phrases like 'the
traditions of Israel' (Judg. 11:39-40) and 'as was the
custom' (Lk. 4:16). Culture is simply a fact of life in the
Bible. It is actually viewed extremely positively at the end
of the Bible where human diversity is a sign of the
effectiveness of the Gospel among the nations. According
to the Revelation, culture will ultimately be celebrated as
ethnicity, languages, people groups and nationalities
become the theme of the biggest party in history. 'You
purchased us for God out of every tribe and language
and people and nation' (Rev. 5:9,14:6).

3. Walk with Christ across cultural lines

The Apostle Paul, like many Muslims today, was brought
up as a bi-cultural person. He was the son of a Pharisee
(Acts 23:6) who was possibly a Jewish immigrant to the
Cilician region of modern-day Turkey (Acts 22:3ff). So
ethnically, culturally and religiously Paul was a devout
Jew (Phil. 3:5). He was privately tutored in the Jewish
equivalent of a Muslim *madrassa* (ultra-orthodox religious
school) in Jerusalem (Acts 22:3). He was also conversant
with the Greek and Italian mindset as a citizen of the
colonial super-power of Rome.

Although the political situation under the Pax Romana
meant that Greek and Latin were the languages of empire,
Paul would have spoken at least four languages including
Hebrew, Aramaic, Latin and Greek. This equipped him in
his work which crossed into several cultures that were
under Roman rule.

If we think of the locations of the churches Paul
founded and wrote letters to, we can imagine how

multi-cultural his work was. Cities such as Ephesus, Colosse and Pisidian Antioch were all in Asia Minor i.e. Turkey; Rome was in what is modern-day Italy; Thessalonica, Philippi and Corinth were all in what is now modern-day Greece; the first Antioch is in modern-day Syria; Illyricum is in modern-day Albania and he also spoke of reaching Spain (Rom. 15:24).

Paul's understanding of apostleship and mission naturally involved crossing ethnic, cultural and linguistic borders. He would say, 'We have received grace and apostleship to call all the Gentiles (the nations AV) to faith and obedience for Jesus Christ's sake' (Rom. 1:5). 'I have a great sense of obligation to people in our culture and to people in other cultures' (Rom. 1:14 NLT). Paul's understanding of church also came out of his cross-cultural mindset which carried over into how he viewed worship. He taught that Christians everywhere need 'all of the Lord's people' (i.e. across the congregation and across the world) in order to comprehend the enormity of God's love (Eph. 3:18).

Paul urged some Greek followers of Jesus at Corinth to serve those outside their cultural group

I make myself a slave to everyone, to win as many as possible. To the Jews I became like a Jew, to win the Jews. To those under the law I became like one under the law . . . To those not having the law I became like one not having the law . . . so as to win those not having the law. . . I have become all things to all men so that by all possible means I might save some. I do all this for the sake of the gospel. . . (1 Cor. 9:19-23) Do not cause anyone to stumble, whether Jews, Greeks or the church of God . . . I try to please everybody in every way . . . that they may be saved. (1 Cor. 10:32-33)

We too face the same challenge to provide a spiritual home and sustenance for people who are following Jesus from non-western backgrounds.

5. When a grace-relationship exists – what next?

'Take fifty thousand people from a wealth of different ethnic backgrounds living within a mile of your church and try to tell them that the message and person of Jesus Christ is relevant to them in their everyday lives.' This is how one minister described the multi-cultural presence in his church's postcode.[5]

The challenge is how to turn the initial relationship into a spiritual friendship. However, the difficulty with many Muslims is their quiet contentment with the spiritual life that is prescribed in Islam so there is little curiosity about how their spiritual hunger might be satisfied. It is always harder to engage with anyone who feels no sense of need; this is the challenge in an affluent and consumerist society too.

Take Ajman in Leicester. He is a gentle, kind Muslim man in his mid-thirties who I met with for some weeks. He told me he was going on *hajj* with his elderly father in January 2005. He seemed totally satisfied with his Islam and did not respond to any leading questions I put. My witness in this situation was limited to what I said and did as a follower of Jesus and the attitude with which I dealt with him, which marked me out from others. Having said that, there was a connection between us which I can water with prayer.

When we find people like Ajman, we need to remove any unhelpful barriers, should they wish to follow Jesus. They need to trust Jesus as their Saviour, have their heart renewed by the Holy Spirit and enter the Kingdom of

God. They do not need to become an adherent of western Christianity or, like Ahmad in chapter three, call themselves 'a Christian'.

The word 'Christian' is a politically loaded word for many Muslims because it provokes negative images of western aggression and other historical baggage dating back many centuries. Although Islamic history is littered with violence committed by Muslims, the fact is that for most Muslims the word 'Christian' has as much emotional appeal as the word 'Nazi' does for British people. So when a Muslim becomes not a Christian but an 'eastern follower of Jesus', they are able to remain longer living for Christ within their own community rather than extracting themselves from it and remaining on the fringe or being expelled.

This is the difference between a New Testament proselyte and a convert. A proselyte merely *transfers* their religious observance of external religious forms from one group to another, whereas the convert has a new life based on an internal relationship with God; this changes the character, form and function of their faith.

Some practical ways to connect naturally with Muslims include:

- running international evenings in your home, church hall or neutral place
- getting prayer requests from Muslims and pray specifically for them
- learning basic vernacular greetings and expressions and using them as appropriate
- visiting Muslim homes with a gift at feast times
- asking what they think of a current event or the radical Muslim element
- running a book table at a local market

- using their business services
- teaching English, especially to women and older men
- running homework clubs for children
- running joint community projects
- greeting them in the street
- setting up a discussion group to share common concerns e.g. law and order, youth problems, secularism and faith.

An extraordinary charity football match was a great success in Leicester when Anglican ministers took on (and lost 5-0) to local imams who were apparently much younger and fitter. To cap it all the referee was an orthodox Jew. This initiative caught the attention of the local media as well as the imagination of a lot of Christians in the area.[6]

A church in the south of England runs a drop-in centre and café for international students where they can meet with friends, practise their English and use the internet. This is attracting Muslims. The life of Jesus is made available on video and DVD and there is strong interest in this. Some students who come from the most restrictive countries of the Muslim world ask for Bibles in their languages.

Churches up and down the UK are offering a practical support service to refugees and asylum seekers. Many of these people are finding their way into the life of these churches at different levels, according to their language ability and situation. Some remain friends of Christians and others become friends of Jesus; both are a result. A reputable resource organization that exists to help Christians interested in this approach is ECSR.[7]

I was invited to speak at Hockley Pentecostal Church in Birmingham with a number of Africans in the congregation. A Nigerian couple wanted their baby dedicated so the church turned the evening into an African theme evening. This included African dress (for those who had it or wanted to wear it) as well as African music and an African meal afterwards. The minister's wife, who was wearing a Nigerian gown, held the baby boy and prayed a moving prayer that God would bless the boy's heritage. The whole evening was a non-patronizing affirmation of the African culture. A Sudanese Muslim background man asked me for an Arabic Bible and six people, mostly African visitors to the church, registered with the minister their decision to follow Christ.

6. Housing Muslim-background people

In order to serve non-western followers of Jesus we need to take our church structures, worship style and content and run these through the grid of the multi-cultural New Testament churches. The following points give us an insight into some core values and activities which provide a bench-mark for good practice such as:

- 'apostolic teaching, fellowship, breaking of bread and prayers' (Acts 2:42)
- group solidarity where the 'believers were together' (Acts 2:44a)
- inter-dependence as 'they had everything in common' (Acts 2:44b)
- access to each others' lives (Col. 3:16)
- commitment to one another including financial support (Acts 2:45)
- shared lives in one another's homes (Acts 2:46)
- participatory group involvement with little hierarchy (1 Cor. 14:26)
- the inclusion (but *not* the domination) of song (Eph. 5:19).

There are three cultural themes that are pertinent for people from Muslim backgrounds. These are:

- *gama'a* (gathering)
- *umma* (community)
- *tariqa* (mentoring).

Any western church wishing to include eastern followers of Jesus within its network of relationships needs to reflect these themes as much as possible both in the life of the 'church gathered' and the 'church scattered' through the week when eastern followers cannot gather with us openly

Gama'a (gathering)
This is the Arabic word for both 'gathering' and 'mosque'. The mosque building is incidental to the Islamic act of 'gathering'. The mosque naturally becomes the hub of Muslim community life because it is the place where friends are met and greeted and everyone is able to catch up on everyone else's news. Even marriages and social contracts are sometimes agreed there. Mosques are therefore the natural meeting point for Muslim communities throughout the week: more like a community centre in western understanding. In gathering, Muslims find a sense of identity, security and support as a minority community in a secular society.

For Muslims, prayer is the primary expression of worship, not singing or preaching, as in Christianity. The mosque is to Islam what the parish church used to be to British culture. Unlike Christians, although a practising Muslim may have a local mosque they prefer, they attend any mosque – especially at *'eid* times when they may go to larger central mosques. For this reason, loyalty to one congregation might not come naturally where there is a choice. This can take time to develop when a Muslim follows Jesus. Another lesson for churches is the need to develop a more 24/7 approach to fellowship and belonging.

Here are some of the problems that were experienced by one such believer who struggled to attach himself to a Sunday morning service in a lively Anglican church in the north of England. He is a Somali called Asmat (name changed). Asmat began to follow Jesus as an asylum-seeker in the UK.

a. Worship

Asmat was uncomfortable with the casual atmosphere, preachers cracking jokes and the use of drama. Interestingly, he found the worship music uplifting – though the church did have exceptionally good musicians.

b. Prayer groups

Asmat found it irrelevant for people to spend a long time getting to know each other and sharing requests, instead of praying. This was partly because his poor English made him feel an outsider which stopped him taking part fully.

c. Security

Somali culture is more secretive than western culture, so persecuted converts like Asmat would be cautious about giving too much away in prayers or testimony. He would just pray for or speak about 'problems' without being specific. Neither did he appreciate being asked probing questions.

d. Distraction

Asmat found worship in a mixed group distracting, especially if there were women who were not modestly dressed (in his view).

e. Legalism

Having moved from the Qur'an to the Bible, Asmat grappled with which items of the Mosaic Law a follower of Jesus should keep and which ones could be dropped and why. Asmat also struggled to accept the Apostle Paul's writings as being of equal authority to Moses so biblical grace was problematic for him.

I am not suggesting that every British church should become unrecognizable in terms of its own 'Britishness' – that would be to lose our own soul; but how could Asmat's needs be better met? Which issues could have been solved by minor adjustments to content and/or structure and which issues could only be met by setting up a parallel context for him to worship in, such as a homegroup or a more formal service? Should it be a parallel non-western style gathering or a specific language group gathering? These are just some of the issues involved in developing a less Anglo-Saxon approach to worship.

2. umma (community)

This means 'family' or 'household'. The term refers to the worldwide community of Islam. The local Muslim community is only a microcosm of the worldwide *umma*. Islam carries with it a corporate mentality. The individual Muslim belongs to the whole. This is why western Muslims react to the plight of Muslim brothers and sisters in Palestine or Iraq. In theory, the Muslim *umma* means that social divides of race and status are blurred in the household of Islam. Muslims feel this most in the *hajj* where a conscious effort is made to this end. Membership of the *umma* fosters a holistic approach to life and faith, which is not just mosque-based.

It is not enough for the local church to offer a surrogate or even an alternative *umma*. The challenge is to be the authentic family of God, for the follower of Jesus from a Muslim background. This is what the Islamic *umma* is aiming at, and what the church is but sometimes struggles to flesh out in practical terms.

3. *tariqa (mentoring)*

This word comes from the Arabic root referring to a 'way' or 'direction'. However, it carries a slightly different meaning in Asian languages such as Urdu. It is an equivalent of the Jewish system of the voluntary pupil to Rabbi relationship. This became reflected in the Christian concept of discipleship.

Muslims want to be spiritually fed and nurtured and loyalty to a chosen teacher is understood. There are particular felt needs experienced by non-western people. These can be discussed as part of the mentoring process. These include the need for power to overcome anxieties; guidance in life decisions; various forms of healing, spiritual protection and even spiritual deliverance.

If multi-cultural church is on God's agenda for a locality we need to be available to him to accomplish it. Culturally inclusive churches are like a dress-rehearsal for the forthcoming multi-cultural carnival in heaven.

The best way to convey the possibilities of such churches is to relate an incident that occurred just after I returned from the Middle East. The incident was not ordinary because it has inspired me for nearly fifteen years, during which time it has been a focus of my prayer and a stimulus which keeps me going on bad days.

Notes

1. Used by H. Jones, *The Muslim Friendly Church* (Kitab Newsletter, May 2005), p1.
2. Brian D. McLaren, *More Ready than You Realize – Evangelism as Dance in the Post-modern Matrix* (Grand Rapids: Zondervan, 2002).
3. Chawkat Moucarry, *Faith to Faith – Christianity and Islam in Dialogue* (Leicester: IVP, 2001), p20.
4. Louis Luzbetek, *The Church and Cultures: An applied anthropology for the religious worker* (Techney, III: Divine Word, 1963), p60-61.
5. Barry Cheeseman (Minister, Ilford High Road Baptist Church), *mh* magazine (July/Aug 1998), p10.
6. *News & Views* – 'The Church of England in Leicestershire, Christians & Muslims Take to the Field' (March 2006), p5.
7. ECSR (Enabling Christians in Serving Refugees).
   The Welcome Centre
   105–107 Maple Road
   London SE20 8LP
   tel: 0208 778 7788
   fax: 0208 778 8811
   email: ecsr@welcomecentre.org
   www.ecsr.org.uk

Postlude
I have a dream

One morning soon after returning to Britain from Egypt my alarm clock brought me hurtling out of a deep sleep. I had been experiencing a vivid dream which had made me cry.

My dream was a visit to a culturally inclusive church where I got a glimpse of the sort of culture-rich environment that is made possible with a little thought and effort. The user-friendly options featured in the dream are real and available to all local churches that are prepared to be flexible enough in their thinking, structure, church programme and the content of their gatherings. Serving God with all our minds means moving beyond merely 'multi-racial' church that is Anglo-Saxon in its worship style; and therefore mono-cultural. The challenge of today is to develop genuinely 'multi-cultural' expressions of worship which touch the heart of non-western people too.

I know of no better way to communicate the culturally-inclusive church concept than through recounting the dream, which may help you grasp it. By sharing this I realize that I am making myself vulnerable because you may feel I am reading too much into a dream; or you may simply reject it as pie-in-the-sky idealism. I am prepared to take that risk.

In my dream . . .

I am being taken by a believer from a Muslim background to a gathering made up of a mixture of people from a spread of ethnic and cultural backgrounds. The meeting is held on a Sunday afternoon in a Community Centre on the edge of a suburban housing estate. People are mingling, some are just standing around or sitting together on easy chairs, while others have taken their shoes off and are sitting cross-legged in a carpeted zone where large cushions and bean-bags are propping them up in comfort.

Finger-food and soft drinks are available, until everyone starts drifting towards the carpeted-zone to claim their places and mode of seating – carpet, cushions, upright or easy chairs. People seem to dress modestly without being old-fashioned. Some are wearing native clothes, either in part or the complete outfit, but I am momentarily distracted by overhearing a variety of greetings – assalâmu alaikum (Arabic), Suber <u>Kh</u>air (Persian), Lebez (North African), izzâyak? (Egyptian) or just Salam (African and Central Asian). The general chatter is in all sorts of languages though the gathering will be run in English, which is common to almost everyone there. I notice groups for interpretation from English being set up around the edges of the room for individuals and clusters of those who need it. This is accepted as the norm rather than a special provision and no one seems to mind the muttering as the session begins.

Young women are clustered together in an area away from the males. Some of the females are wearing either the hijab headscarf or the longer jilbâb shawl. It had never crossed my mind that a Muslima would still wear these Islamic head and body coverings when they follow Jesus. Interpretation is going on into two languages in the female area. One of the translators is an elderly English woman who, I learn later, has been a missionary for twenty-five years and is now retired but still serves the women of one of the ethnic groups represented.

I scan the meeting and notice that people in the carpeted zone have all taken off their shoes, designating it as a holy area. The remainder sit western-style on a mixture of furnishings around the edges of the large carpet and there is an outer cordon of upright chairs for late-comers. The general shape of the gathering is like an elongated lozenge with a racially mixed team of leaders sitting at one end so they can be seen from around the room.

On the walls are removable hangings with Islamic-looking calligraphy. I wonder if some sort of syncretism is going on until I read the Arabic and realize they are from the Bible, not the Qur'an. The quotations have English or French translation underneath.

There is a moment of hushed silence.

The meeting starts, not with a verbal welcome but with a CD being played. The music is soft, stylized and vaguely oriental, yet it could even be Western. Then the meditative atmosphere is broken as one of the cross-legged leaders dramatically and authoritatively recites in Arabic from Isaiah 40, using an eastern carved book-stand on the floor. He savours the beauty and power of the Arabic meaning; a pause – then someone else reads the same passage with rehearsed skill from the English Bible.

After the reading the music fades, and the gathering slips again into a meditative silence. Next, the leading men assume various prayer postures in the carpeted zone. Everyone follows the cue – some standing and extend their forearms at waist height in front of them. Others find space to lean right over and touch the floor with their forehead in biblical prostration. This corporate prayer is spontaneous, with a mixture of fervent Pentecostal-style calling on God and people standing or *silently sitting with outstretched hands. A physical response seems important to most of the group, who fall silent as a leader prays out loud in an Asian language, while someone else translates.*

After the spontaneous praying, the quiet music starts again – I had not noticed it stop. This is apparently a cue for people to sit down. Another leader stands to greet everyone and there follows some sharing of incidents that have happened in the lives of the group. Two of the sharers need interpretation into English. Some of the things are naturally humorous and the response is warm and real, though somehow muted without being restrained. One couple from a situation of persecution in Africa had been burgled so a separate offering is arranged to help them.

The gathering then prays for the African couple, along with on-going issues which concern the group, including a need of healing for one member and the spiritual 'cleansing' of demonic activity in the home of friends of another. Hands are laid on the first and arrangements are made for a team to visit the second. Other bits of news and announcements follow, revealing that the fellowship has a loose link with a church in the area. Then comes the Breaking of Bread in which non-alcoholic wine is used in individual cups. The way this was handled reminds me of the times I have shared the breaking of the fast meal (iftâr) sitting cross-legged with Muslim friends on the floors of British mosques during Ramadan.

After a brief Bible exhortation from another leader – a white guy in a dog-collar – the gathering breaks up and people start drifting back to the refreshments area. The informal parts of the proceedings seem to have lasted longer than the formal part.

Apparently many members of the community no longer observe halal but they do avoid eating pork or drinking alcohol for the sake of their network of Muslim friends. Many prefer to call themselves 'followers of Nabi Isa al-Masih *(the Prophet Jesus Christ) rather than 'Christians.'*

People begin their various leave-taking procedures, which involves prolonged same-gender hugs and kisses, according to their particular cultural background. There is even some handshaking across the gender divide.

Unlike institutional churches, this community defines itself not when 'gathered' but by its network of relationship when 'scattered'. As we leave the Community Centre, I realize that it has taken this sort of community to help my friend Mahmoud find life in Christ and follow him without taking on an unnecessarily western or 'Christian' identity.

This dream is already becoming a reality in Britain as new ways of doing church are being explored. For example, a friend of mine from a Sikh background has started such a culturally inclusive fellowship called 'Sanctuary'. This was launched in Birmingham in 2000 in response to a prophecy that said 'Come to people with a spirit like mine of acceptance, of love, recognize their seeking . . . be gentle, accepting. Do everything out of a motive of love, as I do.' The ethos of Sanctuary has become unconditional love, acceptance and forgiveness for those of other faiths or no faith.

Gatherings are held just outside the Asian community so people can attend without being observed. Many attend wearing ethnic dress and lighting is kept low. This helps to create personal space for private meditation and prayer. Gatherings are kept simple and uncluttered with plenty of opportunity to connect with God in a tranquil atmosphere, helped by eastern décor and gentle Asian music. Candles are also used as a spiritual symbol to represent Jesus as the light that has come into the world. Asian sweets are also eaten during prayer times to symbolize the joy that Jesus brings into our sorrow. Sanctuary provides a 'safe place of grace for east and west to discover Jesus without losing their cultural identity'.[1] May many more such groups emerge.

After speaking at a conference for a major mission organization, I was approached by an Oxford University student. She said that she too had recently had a dream. Her dream was about the Burning Bush as recorded in Exodus chapter three, where Moses was attracted by the flames to go just close enough to the bush in order to hear God call him by name. I agreed with the student that this was precisely the role that God wants western followers of Jesus to play with the Muslim. It is at the heart of the relational witness described throughout this book.

The Apostle Paul advocated the relational approach to Christian witness when he used expressions like 'Christ in you, the hope of glory' (Col. 1:27). This is a reality at the heart of the gospel of grace. It is a profound mystery how and why God wants to recreate in us the *shekinah* (divine luminosity) that graced the heart of the ancient Jewish Tabernacle in the wilderness.

Can we, with a little more humility and Christ-like attractiveness, become such burning bushes that draw Muslim friends just close enough to us to enable them to hear the divine whisper, as God calls them by name, out of a lifestyle under law, into a grace relationship with Himself?

Notes

1. Cuthbert N. and Stoddard C., *Church on Edge* (Milton Keynes: Authentic, 2006). Reviewed in *Inspire* Magazine, July 2006, p22-23. For information on Sanctuary go to www.eastandwest.co.uk.

Appendix
Holy Land – a red herring

The Israeli Wars

First War: 1948 – War of Independence

The formal recognition of the State of Israel triggered a reaction among Arab nations who sided with their Palestinian cousins. Egypt, Iraq, Jordan, Lebanon, Saudi Arabia and Syria declared war on the state of Israel. It was a conflict that became known as the Israeli 'War of Independence' as the baby State fought for its life. The Arab nations attempted to alter the boundaries set by the UN which they saw as an imposition on the region by the West. However, Israel won the war (with the help of God or superior American weaponry or both). The Jews took 77 per cent of the land, which was 33 per cent more than the UN originally awarded.

However, Jordan still occupied the West Bank and East Jerusalem, issuing Jordanian citizenship papers (not passports) to 750,000 Palestinians who fled there. Israel then closed its borders and have prevented displaced Palestinians from returning to their homes ever since. Over 350 villages were destroyed. Theodore Herzl, the founder of political Zionism, had said in his diary as early as 12 June 1895 that the removal of the Arabs bodily from Palestine was part of the plan to 'spirit a penniless population across the frontier by denying it employment. Both the process of expropriation and the removal of the poor must be carried out discreetly and circumspectly.'

Second War: 1956 – Sinai War

Guerrilla warfare rumbled on against the State of Israel for eight years. Then Egypt nationalized the Suez Canal, closing it to Israeli shipping and blockading the Israeli Red Sea port of Eilat. Israel then attacked Egypt overland across the Sinai desert as the British and the French bombed Port Said and Port Fu'ad. Only UN condemnation and pressure from the US government restored order.

Third War: 1967 – Six Day War

Border skirmishes continued between Israel and Syria, Jordan and Egypt. The tension escalated again until Egypt demanded that UN troops be withdrawn from its territory in Sinai. It then proceeded to blockade Eilat again. Israel retaliated with an air strike that virtually wiped out the Egyptian air force on the ground. Within a week, Israel had added to its territories East Jerusalem, the Sinai, Gaza, the West Bank and the Golan Heights.

This led to a further wave of refugee movement as Arabs fled these newly occupied areas. The UN issued its famous Resolution 242 ordering Israel to return land and retreat to its 1967 borders – this is cited to this day as the unfulfilled Resolution.

Fourth War: 1973 – Yom Kippur War

Israel basked in its victory while Arab pride was bruised. Egypt took Israel by surprise on the religious festival of Yom Kippur (Day of Atonement). On this national Bank Holiday, Israel's new border with Egypt was overrun. It took American satellite intelligence on tank movements and the provision of superior weaponry for Israel to be able to fight back and win.

Fifth War: 1982 – Invasion of Lebanon

Exiled Palestinians mounted a guerrilla campaign into north Galilee. Israel retaliated and launched an all-out attack to establish a buffer zone which it could control with the help of Lebanese Christian militiamen. These men were also used later in terrorist attacks on the Palestinian refugee camps of Sabra and Shatila until all the Palestine Liberation Organization (PLO) activists in Lebanon were escorted out of the country and given safe passage to Tunisia. The PLO offices in Tunis were later bombed by Israel.

Sixth War: 1987–93 – Intifada

The Arab states began to accept the fact of the State of Israel as a new generation grew up in Palestine which had only known life under the status quo of occupation. It is this generation that has led the popular uprising as a struggle towards a just solution to the problem of a homeland for Palestinians. The word *intifada* means to 'shake off aggressively' like the Apostle Paul shaking off the snake that bit him and clung to his hand on a Malta beach (Acts 28:3-6).

During the *intifada* period many Palestinian 'martyrs' died in brutal suicide attacks on innocent Jews provoking violent retaliation from the Israeli army in which 1,392

Palestinians were killed by shooting, beating or teargas (230 of the dead were under sixteen years old); 16,000 were imprisoned; 1,882 homes demolished and 382 homes sealed shut; 25,000 Palestinians were put under daily curfew and 130,787 were injured as a result of Israeli military action.

For further reading on Israel and Palestine, I recommend the following:

Gary Burge, *Whose land? Whose promise?* (Carlisle: Paternoster Press, 2003)

Colin Chapman, *Whose holy city?* (Oxford: Lion Hudson, 2004)

Thomas Friedman, *From Beirut to Jerusalem* (HarperCollins, 1998)

Anton La Guardia, *Holy Land, Unholy War* (London: John Murray, 2002)

* * * *

Steve Bell can be contacted by e-mail on sbell2101@aol.com or via www.friendshipfirst.org

Steve's best-selling manual *Friendship First* describes how ordinary Christians can relate to ordinary Muslims. It is available as follows:

Inside the UK, by cheque c/o Steve Bell (e-mail address as above)

Worldwide, by credit card from . . .
c/o Advance Bookshop
17 Monks Road
Lincoln
LN2 5HL
Tel: 01522 525898
e-mail: mail@advancebookshop.co.uk
www.advancebookshop.co.uk